VAULT.COM
> the insider career network™

VAULT.COM GUIDE TO THE CASE INTERVIEW

VAULT.COM GUIDE TO THE CASE INTERVIEW

MARK ASHER AND THE STAFF OF VAULT.COM

For information about permission to reproduce selections from this book, contact Vault.com Inc., P.O. Box 1772, New York, New York 10011-1772, (212) 366-4212.

Library of Congress CIP Data is available.

ISBN 1-58131-122-2

Printed in the United States of America

ACKNOWLEDGEMENTS

Vault.com would like to acknowledge the assistance and support of Geoff Baum, Ken Cron, Matt Doull, Glenn Fischer, Mark Hernandez, Ravi Mhatre, Tom Phillips, Jay Oyakawa, Carter Weiss, the folks at Hollinger Ventures, Ingram, and Globix, and our families and friends

This book is dedicated to consultants and consulting candidates everywhere. Good luck.

willing to pay $120K

[asking for $80K]

www.Vault.com   AOL Keyword: Vault.com

Industry Channels

Insider Research > Compensation

Message Boards

News

Find a Job

Resources and insights, from
"Am I Worthy" to message
boards so you can know what
you're really worth.

VAULT.COM

> the insider career network

[The truth is in the VAULT]

Shouldn't your future be as bright as you are?

What are you going to do about it?

As a leader in driving radical transformation in the private and public sectors, AMS is looking for a certain kind of person. We are at the forefront of transforming industries that crave high-impact IT solutions, so we need individuals who are hungry for the opportunity to build their personal portfolios of challenging experiences. We need motivated people who are willing to work hard and accept the responsibility of determining how rapidly they advance. We need people like you. What are you going to do about it?

ams.com

INTRODUCTION 1

CASE STRATEGIES

CASE FRAMEWORKS

Hungry for more inside scoop? Join Vault.com's popular
online community for consulting — www.vault.com

VAULT.com   **xi**

BEING THERE

REAL LIFE INTERVIEWS

BUSINESS CASES

GUESSTIMATES

BRAINTEASERS

FINAL ANALYSIS   142

APPENDIX

Hungry for more inside scoop? Join Vault.com's popular
online community for consulting — www.vault.com

VAULT.com   **xiii**

INTRODUCTION

Why the case?

Your impressive resume may get you an interview with a consulting firm, but it won't get you the job. Consultants know that a resume, at its very best, is only a two-dimensional representation of a multi-faceted, dynamic person.

And because consulting firms depend on employing those multi-faceted, dynamic people, the firms rely heavily on the case interview to screen candidates. The interview process is especially pertinent in the consulting industry since consulting professionals spend the lion's share of their business day interacting with clients and colleagues, and must themselves constantly interview client employees and executives.

Furthermore, consultants must have a select set of personality and leadership traits in order to be successful. A consultant's work environment is extremely turbulent. There are nonstop engagement team changes, hostile client environments, countless political influences, and near-perpetual travel. These factors dictate that an individual be cool under pressure, be influential without being condescending, be highly analytical, have the ability to understand the granular aspects of a problem while simultaneously aggregating them to see the big picture, and have the ability to self-police a balance between personal and professional lifestyle.

Consultants are often staffed in small groups in far-flung areas. As a result, the individual must be able to function, and function well, without many of the traditional workplace standards: a permanent working space, the ability to return home each night, easily accessed services such as administrative assistance, faxing, and photocopying, and the camaraderie that develops among co-workers assigned to the same business unit.

All these factors necessitate a unique interview structure focused on assessing a candidate's ability to manage these particular circumstances with professionalism and excellence. The case interview has evolved as a method for evaluating these characteristics.

WHAT IS A CASE?

Simply put, a case interview is the analysis of a business question. Unlike most other interview questions, it is an interactive process. Your interviewer will present you with a business problem and ask you for your opinion. Your job is to ask the interviewer logical questions that will permit you to make a detailed recommendation. The majority of case interviewers don't have a specific answer that you, the candidate, are expected to give. What the interviewer is looking for is a thought process that is at once analytical and creative (what consultants love to call "out-of-the-box" thinking). Specific knowledge of the industry in question is a bonus but not necessary. Business school students and candidates with significant business world experience receive case questions that require a deeper understanding of business models and processes.

The interview with a consulting company normally lasts about half an hour. Of this time, about 10 to 20 minutes is taken up with preliminary chat and behavioral questions and five minutes of your asking questions about the company. This leaves 5 to 15 minutes for your case interview question or questions. Make them count!

Types of case interviews

What case interviews are not designed to do is to explore educational, professional, or experiential qualifications. If you've reached the case interview stage, take a deep breath – the consulting firm has already weighed your background, GPA, and experience and found you worthy of a deeper skill assessment. This means that the case interview is yours to lose. Triumph over your case interviews and chances are that a slot at the firm will open for you.

Case interviews vary widely, but in general they fall into three groups: business cases, guesstimates, and brainteasers. These questions are designed to assess a particular set of candidate characteristics that an individual would be required to possess as part of the tactical and/or lifestyle aspects of being a consultant.

Case interviews

Case interviews vary somewhat in their format. The classic and most common type of case interview is the business case, in which you're presented with a business scenario and asked to analyze it and make recommendations. Most cases are presented in oral form, though some involve handouts, and a few (like Monitor Company's) are entirely written. (That is, the interviewer will not contribute any other information besides what's on the handout.) Another variation on the case interview that is becoming more popular is the group case interview, where three to six candidates are grouped together and told to solve a case cooperatively. Consultants from the firm watch as silent observers. Though

Hungry for more inside scoop? Join Vault.com's popular
online community for consulting — www.vault.com

VAULT.COM   **3**

you should certainly be prepared for these variations on case interviews, you are most likely to come across the traditional, *mano-a-mano* case interview.

Guesstimates

Whether free-standing or as part of a case, learning how to make "back-of-the-envelope" calculations (rough, yet basically accurate) is an essential part of the case interview. As part of a guesstimate, you might be asked to estimate how many watermelons are sold in the United States each year, or what the market size for a new computer program that organizes your wardrobe might be. (For example, you might need to figure out the market size for the wardrobe software as a first step in determining how to enter the European market.) You will not be expected to get the exact number, but you should come close – hence the guesstimate. Non-business school students and others who appear to be weak quantitatively may get stand-alone guesstimates – guesstimates given independently of a case.

Brainteasers

Brainteasers are normally logic puzzles or riddles. They may be timed. Often, brainteasers are meant to test both analytic and "out-of-the-box" thinking, as well as grace under pressure.

Skills assessed in the case interview

Following your case interview, your consulting interviewer will complete a written evaluation form. The evaluation forms often include a list of qualities, traits, and abilities, and ask the interviewer to assess the candidate against the list. Following is a list of these special traits that, according to consulting insiders, interviewers will be keeping an eye out for as you work through the case interview:

Leadership skills

You'll hear this from every consulting firm out there – they want leaders. Why, you might ask, would a consulting firm need a leader? After all, many beginning consultants are consigned to independent number-crunching and research. The fact is, however, that consultants are often called upon to work independently, shape projects with very little direction, and direct others. You should demonstrate your leadership skills by taking charge of the case interview. Ask your questions confidently. Inquire whether the case interview relates to the interviewer's own experience. While your resume and previous leadership experience will probably most strongly convey your leadership ability, your demeanor in the case interview can help.

Analytical skills

The core competency of consulting is analysis – breaking down data, formulating it into a pattern that makes sense, and deriving a sensible conclusion or recommendation. You should display this skill through your efficient, on-target, and accurate questions while wrestling your case to a solution.

Presentation skills

The case presentation is an essential part of consulting. Once consultants have analyzed their case engagement and decided on the proper course of action, they must present their findings and recommendations to their case team and to their clients. Interviewers will be watching you closely to see if you stumble over words, use inadvisable fillers like "um" or "like" frequently, or appear jittery under close questioning. Remember: When you're speaking, slow down and smile. If asked a question that temporarily stumps you, take a deep breath and pause. It's always better to pause than babble.

Energy

Even the most qualified and analytical consultant won't be much good if she quits at 5 p.m. during a long and arduous engagement. Interviewers look for zest and energy – firm handshake, sincere and warm smile, bright eyes, and bushy tail. Remember that consulting firms expect you to take a 10-hour flight and show up at work the next day alert, perky, and ready to go.

Attention to detail/Organization

Consultants must be as painstaking as scientists in their attention to detail. And consultants who juggle two or more flights a week and engagements all over the world must be extremely organized. You can display this skill through a disciplined, logical approach to your case solution, and by showing up for your interview prepared. You'll want to take notes, so bring a pad of paper and a pen. Interviewers notice when candidates must ask for these materials.

Quantitative skills

Those spreadsheets you'll be working with as a management consultant need numbers to fill them. Consulting interviews will inevitably test your grasp of numbers and your ability to manipulate them. Many interviewers will assess your quantitative skills by giving you a "guesstimate," either within the case question or separately.

Flexibility

Consultants may have to arrive at the office one day and be packed off to Winnipeg for six months the next. This kind of flexibility of schedule is mirrored

Hungry for more inside scoop? Join Vault.com's popular
online community for consulting — www.vault.com

VAULT.com   **5**

in tests for mental flexibility. To test your grasp of a case interview, the interviewer may suddenly introduce a new piece of information ("Okay, let's say the factories must be opened either in Canada or China") or flip the terms of the case interview ("What if this labor contract is not guaranteed, as I said earlier?") and then watch how quickly you're able to alter your thinking.

Maturity

Consultants must often work with executives and company officials decades older than they are. (This is why consultants are taught the right way to answer the question, "How old are you?") What this means in an interview is a minimum of giggling, fidgeting, and references to awesome fraternity events you may have attended, even if the interviewer seems receptive.

Intelligence, a.k.a. "mental horsepower"

Rather straightforward – consulting interviewers are looking for quickness of analysis and depth of insight. Don't be afraid to ask questions for fear of looking stupid – smart people learn by asking questions and assimilating new information. At the same time, asking your interviewer to repeat an elementary (or irrelevant) concept 20 times will not burnish your image.

What kind of case will I get?

While there's no way to tell for sure what case question you'll get, there are some things that can tip you off to the kind of case you'll receive.

If you're an undergraduate or other non-MBA student, you can probably be safely assured of getting a creative or "open-ended" question. "We don't expect our undergraduate candidates to know that much about business," confides one interviewer. "What we do expect is the ability to break down and articulate complex concepts." Undergraduates are also much more likely to get guesstimates and brainteasers than MBAs.

Are you a business school student or graduate? Then your case question will probably be less open-ended, and drive toward an actual solution. Your interviewer may posit something from her own experience – knowing what course of action the consultancy actually ended up recommending. This doesn't mean you have to make the same recommendation – but you'd better be able to back up your reasoning! Alternatively, one thing case interviewers love to do is look at your resume and give you a case question that relates to your past experience. "For example," says one consultant, "if you were on the advertising staff for the school newspaper, you might be given a question about investing in advertising agencies." For this reason, advise consultants, "it makes sense to follow up on your field in *The Wall Street Journal* because you may be asked about recent developments in it. If you know what's going on you'll be that much more impressive." Some guesstimates, for example, figuring out the total worldwide revenues of *Tarzan*, are broad enough so that most people can make a reasonable assumption of numbers.

Hungry for more inside scoop? Join Vault.com's popular
online community for consulting — www.vault.com

V/\ULT.com   **7**

VAULT.com

CASE
STRATEGIES

Your objective

Business cases involve real-world situations for which a candidate is provided with a set of facts about a business or business problem. Business cases can be presented as a narrative detailed by the interviewer (most common) or on paper. They may also take the form of a case study, where the candidate is presented with a packet of text including graphs, charts, financial information, and other exhibits.

Regardless of the format, the objective of the business case remains the same. The interviewer is attempting to assess your ability to synthesize many different situational elements into a cohesive understanding of the problem at hand. As a candidate, you will need to draw upon your analytical abilities, business experience, and deductive reasoning to crack the case. In most cases, the business case will be timed, and can last anywhere from 15 minutes to an hour. (While you will usually be given only one case in an interview, you may be given two or more shorter cases.)

In some situations, business cases may be presented with little or no information. The interviewer may simply toss out a few facts like, "We have a multi-billion dollar consumer products client with operations in 15 countries. What would you advise them?" Then the interviewer falls silent. In addition to appraising the aforementioned skills, the interviewer may deliberately choose this vagueness to assess a candidate's poise, reaction to an unfamiliar situation, overall confidence, and grace under pressure.

Don't fret!

There are no "correct" answers to business case questions. In fact, many times you will not reach a conclusion before the interviewer moves on to other questions. This is not a sign that something has gone terribly wrong. The interviewer is not looking for a definitive answer, rather he is assessing your ability to analyze and synthesize various facts, clarify the situation, and set up a framework for pursuing other information. If you have already successfully demonstrated that you have the capability to perform these tasks, your interviewer may wish to move on to a different subject or case. In fact, if the interviewer moves on to another case, it shows that you're still a viable candidate. If you've screwed up," states an interviewer, "they'll probably just spend the rest of the time on chit chat."

Top 10 tips for answering business case questions successfully

1. Take notes

As your interviewer presents your case, be sure to take careful notes on the numbers or other facts given. (Always bring a notepad and a pen to a consulting interview.) If you plan on drawing graphs, add brownie points by bringing graph paper (which shows major foresight). You don't want to be put in the position of asking your interviewer to later repeat information.

2. Make no assumptions

As a case interviewee, you should never make any assumptions. Your interviewer will inevitably leave things out of the case presented to you. (If an apple juice manufacturer has seen its expenses rise dramatically, for example, your interviewer probably won't mention the tree blight that's constricting the supply of apples.) You should assume the persona of an actual consultant trying to learn about an assignment. It might seem obvious that there is no pre-existing workplan (because if there was, why would this be a case interview?) but you may want to ask. You should also ask if the company has encountered a similar problem, or what other companies in the field have done when faced with similar situations. Your interviewer may not release that information but will be impressed that you asked these sensible questions. Some good basic "professional" questions to ask, which apply to most cases:

- What is the product?

- Who hired us?

- How long will this engagement last?

- Is there a workplan?

- Has the company faced this problem (or opportunity) before? If so, how did it react? What was the outcome?

- What have other companies facing this situation done?

- Has the firm already done any research into the issue? If so, what were its findings?

3. Ask questions

Your interviewer expects you to ask questions – as many intelligent questions as you need to obtain an accurate picture of the relevant facts in the case.

Hungry for more inside scoop? Join Vault.com's popular
online community for consulting — www.vault.com

VAULT.com **11**

Many inexperienced case interviewees make the error of asking their interviewer too few questions. They may be afraid that they will look ignorant, or not wish to "bother" the interviewer. Remember – not asking questions is a fatal error in a case interview. If you don't know the first thing about the helicopter market, ask how much it costs to manufacture a rotor. If you need to estimate the demand for a beef-flavored potato snack in Wichita, Kansas, then feel free to ask the population of Wichita and environs.

You will often find that your interviewer will direct your line of questioning to a specific area, but you must always be ready to control the conversation in case the interviewer does not direct your reasoning. If you are unsure, simply ask the interviewer. For instance, if you find the interviewer offering little direction as you move through your initial questions, you may wish to ask, "I find the lack of a risk assessment to be a potential showstopper. Might I ask some detailed questions about this?" Or you might say, "Given what you have told me about the situation, I would like to find out more about the client's current relationship with its distribution partner. Would that be OK?" In this way, you take charge of the line of questioning without stepping on the interviewer's role.

4. Listen to the answers you get

One interviewer warns: "Many candidates get so caught up in asking the perfect questions that they don't listen to the answers they receive. They go through a mental list of all the questions they want to ask, and ignore the response they got. That throws off their reasoning." Make sure you respond to the information you receive.

5. Maintain eye contact

Always maintain direct eye contact during the case interview. Eye contact is critical when answering case questions – it demonstrates confidence and authority. Remember that in consulting you may find yourself in front of 20 executives at a major corporation presenting a strategy you were briefed on only a half-hour ago. And then you have to answer questions! So you can see why business case interviewing is so important to consulting – it simulates the work environment consultants must face every day.

6. Take your time

It's perfectly fine to take a minute to think through your answer – in fact, most interviewers find it preferable. "Whenever I asked to take the time out to collect my thoughts," reports one consultant who's undergone "dozens" of case interviews, "my interviewers always said 'Okay, good, go ahead.'" On the other hand, while "a minute of deep thinking" is fine, "five minutes is really overkill. You don't want your interviewer waiting there for five minutes. The case is only supposed to be 15 or 20 minutes."

7. Lay out a road map for your interviewer

After you've selected your approach, don't keep it a secret. Tell your interviewer what approach you're going to take. For example, you might say, "First, I'm going to discuss the Mexican and Canadian markets. Second, I'll ask about our entry strategy. Finally, I'm making a recommendation." "One of the most important things consultants have to do is present complex ideas in a lucid manner," explains one interviewer. "That's why you should take time to explain your reasoning. Not only will it impress your interviewer and allow you to confirm any assumption that you're making, but it will allow you to get your own thinking straight."

8. Think out loud

In order to navigate case interviews (successfully), you will need to act quickly and confidently. The business case is an opportunity to show the interviewer how you think. Your interviewer wants to know that you can reason in a rapid and logical fashion. As you assess, compile, and analyze the elements presented to you, be sure that you speak aloud and explain your reasoning. This is the only way the interviewer can assess your performance.

You may not be entirely comfortable thinking out loud. So if you're not feeling confident thinking aloud, try practicing by yourself. Start with something simple like explaining aloud to yourself how to change a tire or how you brush your teeth. Minimize "ums" and other fillers, so that what you say is concise, direct, and clear.

Next, try practicing on friends or family. Have them ask questions for which you must assess a situation. For example, they might ask, "I'm not sure at which bank I should open a checking account. What are the trade-offs between Bank X and Bank Y?" or "I've got $50 to spend on groceries, so what should I buy?" Even speaking to yourself in front of the mirror will build your confidence thinking "on the fly" while simultaneously speaking.

Hungry for more inside scoop? Join Vault.com's popular
online community for consulting — www.vault.com

VAULT.com   **13**

9. **Present your thinking in a clear, logical manner. Where useful, use frameworks and business concepts to organize your answer.**

   You should develop a framework for assessing case interview questions which can be applied to different situations. In general, in any situation you will want to:

   - Understand the scope of the engagement

   - Pinpoint the objectives

   - Identify the key players

   Beyond this, you may choose any line of questioning or structure with which you feel comfortable. As you practice, you will find yourself developing this framework unconsciously as you attempt to gain clarity over a situation. Capture and package this framework, and have it available by memory (or on paper if you wish) for use at any time.

   Where useful, also use advanced business concepts and frameworks – such as Porter's Five Forces or Value Chain Analysis – (see the chapter on case frameworks) to help organize your thoughts and impress your interviewer.

10. **Quickly summarize your conclusions**

    You have limited time in your case interview to make your point. If you are uncomfortable with quickly summarizing your conclusions, think about being faced with this classic situation:

    "A consultant working for a multinational corporation inadvertently bumped into the CEO of the corporation while waiting for the elevator. As they got on the elevator, the CEO announced that he was on his way to a Board of Directors meeting on the 34th floor. He then instructed the consultant to brief him completely on the major findings of the project in the time it took the elevator to go from the 1st floor to the 34th floor."

    While this is no doubt an urban legend, it is extremely likely that you will encounter time-pressured situations many times in your professional career, especially in consulting, where time is a precious commodity. If you are taking a while reaching your conclusion, your interviewer may ask you for the "60 second pitch." Practice summarizing your answer in a minute or less.

WHAT IF I GET ONE OF THOSE GROUP CASE INTERVIEWS?

While Monitor used to be one of a very few consulting companies that gave a group case interview, its popularity is increasing. In a group interview, between two and five candidates are given a case and asked to present their findings in one hour. A few consultants from the firm remain with the candidates to silently observe their progress.

One important thing to remember is that the group interview is not a zero sum game. "Everyone may get an offer, or no one may get an offer," confirms one consultant. The key with group case interviews is to show your keen organizational and teamwork abilities. Don't bully your fellow candidates, but don't sit back and quietly do as you are told. One recent group case interviewee suggests, "Present your thoughts on how to divide the analysis. Listen to what others have to say. Try to determine areas of expertise. If you disagree with their thoughts or estimates, say so, but never be denigrating or rude. Look like you're having a good time. Otherwise, the analysis is pretty similar to a regular case."

Common problems and troubleshooting

Even though the case interview isn't designed to stress you out (brainteasers are another story), invariably, consulting candidates get nervous during their interviews. "Even MBAs get nervous," says one business school student. "You're really on the spot and you keep thinking about the job."

But, say recent interviewees, don't be so stressed that you assume that you're doomed. "A lot of times, you'll make a recommendation, and the interviewer will start arguing for another outcome. They are just doing that to see if you stick to your guns." On the other hand, if you've done an analysis based on an assumption that is blatantly wrong, and the interviewer makes this point to you – "Well, don't you think your estimation of the annual consumption of electric blankets in the United States as 3 billion is a bit high, considering there are only 275 million people in the country?" – don't blindly stick to a flawed conclusion.

In fact, it's pretty normal to make erroneous assumptions or conclusions during the case interview. One consultant says: "One of the most common mistakes case interviewees make is to screw up once and then freeze. They assume that they've irrevocably ruined their chances at the firm. But in fact, learning from mistakes is a big part of being a consultant. The interviewer will be impressed

Hungry for more inside scoop? Join Vault.com's popular
online community for consulting — www.vault.com

VAULT.com   **15**

if the candidate can rebound." "If you go the wrong way, it doesn't necessarily result in a ding," confirms another consultant. "Most interviewers will try to lead you back to the true path. If you can pick up on this and follow their lead you will still be in the running."

Thinking about the case

Many business case questions ask you to do some form of "reasoning" or logic thought process. Here are some types of business case questioning with which you should become familiar. While not exhaustive, many business case questions fall into these general categories of thought process:

- **Weigh the pros and cons** – You will be asked to identify and describe the various trade-offs between two or more choices.

- **Break down a complex system** – Given a large multi-faceted problem, sort the problem's pieces into distinct elements and articulate the overall nature of the issue.

- **Resolve a conflict** – When presented with a situation in which two or more elements are in direct dispute or opposition, you will be asked to develop a framework for resolution. There may be no "correct" answer; you must argue successfully for your conclusion.

- **Interpret the numbers** – You will be presented with a series of financial or other quantitative exhibits and be asked to develop and articulate a synthesis of this information, which may involve some basic conclusions (but not necessarily an answer to the problem).

- **Fill in the blanks** – The interviewer will provide you with minimal information. You will be expected to scope the situation through a dialogue with the interviewer and then most probably address one of the other categories listed above.

The case checklist

You may be able to tell the difference between the 4 Cs and the 4 Ps, but don't get so hung up on memorizing frameworks that you forget some basic steps that can make the difference between a great case and one that goes less than smoothly.

Before the case

Arrive on time. Time is money for consultants. If you keep your interviewer waiting, will you also keep clients waiting as well?

Take time to assess your surroundings. Remember, interviews aren't a one-way process. If you're uncomfortable in the office, that's not a good sign.

Dress appropriately. It bears repeating that even though most consulting firms have gone business casual, you should still wear a suit for your interview.

Bring the following items with you: a pen, a watch, a pencil, a pad of paper, some graph paper, and a calculator. You may not be allowed to use the calculator, but if you are, you'll be glad you brought one.

During the case

Don't ignore the chitchat. Your interviewer is evaluating you on your potential for poise and teamwork as well as sheer mental horsepower.

Be consistent, but not monotonous. In most consulting firms, interviewers keep notes on what they talked to you about, what you talked about, and your strengths and weaknesses. If you have one joke that you like to tell or one story about your great leadership ability, it'll wear a little thin (in the eyes of your interviewers). At the same time, your interviewers will note inconsistencies in statements that you make.

Take notes when your interviewer is describing the case. Otherwise, you may miss important points.

Repeat the case back. This will both concentrate your mind and let you know if you've conceptualized the case correctly.

Don't be afraid to ask for help — but phrase your questions in the form of a statement (just think — the opposite of Jeopardy.) If you're having trouble interpreting a graph, say "I would interpret these numbers as stating that the cost of our production of widgets is rising rapidly. Am I on the right track here?) Your interviewer will be more likely to help you than if you stare at her blankly and plead for mercy.

Hungry for more inside scoop? Join Vault.com's popular
online community for consulting — www.vault.com

VAULT.com **17**

If you screw up, don't panic. "You can mess up an interview and still get the job," advises one consultant. Remain calm — and ask for pointers on where you went wrong. Consultants like people who ask questions.

After the case

Send thank you notes — the sooner the better. E-mail works, and works even better if you remember specific things about the interview.

Watch your mouth! Never discuss a case while you're still in the office — wait until you're at home with friends. If you're taken out to lunch or are sitting in the lobby of the firm, you're still on interview. Some firms even ask their alumni for assessments of candidates — so that ex-McKinsey consultant next to you in your class may be asked to assess you.

Specific types of business cases

Many business cases can be categorized as one of the following eight common "types" of business cases. Some may be combinations of two or three case types, or require you to solve problems that fall into different categories.

Falling Profits Case

- **In a nutshell:** This type of case asks you to explore the possible reasons behind a company's drop in profits.

- **What this type of question is designed to assess:** Analytical ability, drilldown from a high-level statement, understanding of financial instruments, communication, industry knowledge

- **Useful concepts/frameworks:** Market assessment, BCG matrix, product mix assessment

- **Some examples of falling profits cases:**

> **Bunny New Media is an Internet content provider that has had three straight quarters of high profit gains, followed by a 50% drop in profits this quarter. What has happened?**

> **Hill Construction has been under contract with the City of Los Angeles to build a new subway station. However, Hill's latest financial statement shows a steep decline in profits relative to this time last year. What is the cause of this decline?**

New Product Introduction

- **In a nutshell:** This type of case asks you to recommend a strategy for introducing a new product.

- **What this type of question is designed to assess:** Analytical ability, understanding of brand management, supply chain, communication, industry knowledge

- **Useful concepts/frameworks:** Four Ps, market analysis, competitor analysis, product portfolio assessment

Hungry for more inside scoop? Join Vault.com's popular
online community for consulting — www.vault.com

VAULT.com   **19**

• **Some examples of new profit product introduction:**

> **Joe's Aircraft Engines has a new design ready for market. How should they pursue this?**

> **Microvilla Software has a new kitchen design application they would like to market over the Internet. How should they go about this?**

Entering a New Market

• **In a nutshell:** This type of case asks you to analyze whether a company should enter a new market or develop a new line of products or services. (Usually, the new products or services are somehow related to the company's current business.)

• **What this type of question is designed to assess:** Analytical ability, understanding of market dynamics, supply chain dynamics, communication, industry knowledge

• **Useful concepts/frameworks:** Market assessment, product portfolio analysis

• **Some examples of new market questions:**

> **Hasma Systems, Inc. currently assembles laser printers for several major high-tech companies. One of these companies has approached you about manufacturing calculators and has asked you to provide an analysis of their ability to provide this service. How would you go about your analysis?**

> **A major consumer products manufacturer currently makes soap, detergent, and canned meat products. Most of the company's product portfolio is considered mature, and it has identified two companies for acquisition: one makes frozen juice concentrate, the other makes hair care products. How would you decide which acquisition, if either, is best for the company?**

Entering a New Geographic Market

- **In a nutshell:** This type of case asks you to analyze whether a company should expand into a new country or region.

- **What this type of question is designed to assess:** Analytical ability, understanding of global market dynamics, geographic currency issues, supply chain dynamics, communication, industry knowledge

- **Useful concepts/frameworks:** Market assessment, supply chain analysis, competitor analysis

- **Some examples of new geographic market questions:**

> **Miller's Wheat Bran wants to introduce its line of bran products in India. How would they go about assessing the feasibility of this idea?**

> **Billy Bo Bob's Chili is the number one chili product in Texas and Oklahoma. The company is interested in introducing their product in California. How would you recommend the company proceed?**

Where to Locate a New Facility ["Site Selection Case"]

- **In a nutshell:** The site selection case asks you to evaluate where a company should locate a new plant or other facility (and sometimes, whether the company's entire operations should be relocated).

- **What this type of question is designed to assess:** Analytical ability, understanding of global market dynamics, regulatory environment, import/export environment, supply chain dynamics, communication, industry knowledge

- **Useful concepts/frameworks:** Market assessment, supply chain analysis, competitor analysis

- **Some examples of site selection cases:**

> **Yaya Manufacturing assembles bicycles exclusively in the United States. Due to cost pressures, the company is thinking of moving operations to Mexico. What factors would you consider in making this decision?**

Hungry for more inside scoop? Join Vault.com's popular
online community for consulting — www.vault.com

VAULT.com **21**

> **A major beverage manufacturer is negotiating with the Indian government to sell its products in India. The government has demanded that the company sell only products made in India, with the added specification that the company open bottling plants in India. What factors should you consider in evaluating this requirement?**

Mergers & Acquisitions Case

- **In a nutshell:** The M&A case asks you to determine whether a particular acquisition would be advisable.

- **What this type of question is designed to assess:** Analytical ability, regulatory environment, supply chain dynamics, communication, industry knowledge

- **Useful concepts/frameworks:** Market assessment, supply chain analysis, competitor analysis, structural analysis

- **Some examples of M&A cases:**

> **Club Med is considering the acquisition of a major cruise line. Describe the way you might assess the viability of this decision.**

> **A software company is interested in acquiring a logistics company to compress their supply chain and reduce their cycle time from manufacturer to retailer. What factors would you consider in determining whether this would be an appropriate decision?**

Competitive Response Case

- **In a nutshell:** A competitive response case asks you to recommend how your client should react to a move by its competitor.

- **What this type of question is designed to assess:** Analytical ability, supply chain dynamics, communication, industry knowledge, market dynamics

- **Useful concepts/frameworks:** Market assessment, supply chain analysis, competitor analysis, structural analysis

• **More competitive response questions:**

> So Pretty Cosmetics sells products only through major department stores. Their major competitor, Porter Cosmetics, has just announced the opening of 10 stand-alone stores. How should So Pretty Cosmetics react?

> Starstruck Video rents and sells video tapes. They have just learned that their competitor, Vader Video, has signed an exclusive deal with Warner Bros. which gives them exclusive rights to offer Warner Brothers videos for 30 days before Starstruck is allowed to offer them. How should Starstruck Video react?

Changes in Government/Regulatory Environment

• **In a nutshell:** This type of case presents a change in the governmental or regulatory environment (for example, a change in the laws of a particular country where a company has operations) and asks you to advise your client.

• **What this type of question is designed to assess:** Analytical ability, supply chain dynamics, communication, industry knowledge, market dynamics, regulatory environment

• **Useful concepts/frameworks:** Market assessment, supply chain analysis, competitor analysis, structural analysis, regulatory analysis

• **Some examples of change in environment questions:**

> La Piñata Inc. manufactures party supplies in Malaysia. The recent currency upheavals in Asia have caused the Malaysian government to impose heavy tariffs on all exports. What should La Piñata do?

> TSC Software is looking to hire 25 software developers from Asia. They are interested in understanding how they might employ these people without asking them to emigrate or importing them as foreign nationals. How would you investigate this?

Hungry for more inside scoop? Join Vault.com's popular
online community for consulting — www.vault.com

VAULT.com   23

CASE
FRAMEWORKS

While you are strongly encouraged to develop your own personal method for understanding and answering case questions, there are some classic models and business concepts that you will find useful in structuring your thinking. "The model and concepts are like a basic recipe," says one consultant. "Any creativity or alteration you make to that model is like seasoning. Your audience – the interviewer – will appreciate it." So here's your cookbook!

We've divided the concepts and frameworks you should know into two levels: basic and advanced. At a minimum, your consulting interviewer will expect you to know the basic concepts and frameworks, even if you have a limited business background. Those with a strong business background (including MBAs) will be expected to have a strong grasp of the advanced concepts as well.

We must remind you that case frameworks are just that – frameworks, not a solution in of themselves. Don't tell your interviewer "I'm going to use the 4Cs." Just do it!

A special note about the Internet and cases
Consultants are increasingly setting their cases in the past – 1985, 1969, or what have you. The reason is to avoid the use of the Internet as a consideration in business cases.

On the other hand, e-consultants may expect you to propose solutions such as B2B marketplaces.

Basic Concepts and Frameworks

These "starter" concepts are useful touchstones for undergrads and others without significant business experience. They allow you to structure your thinking in the way a consultant's business-minded clients would expect.

Cost-benefit analysis — *Pro or Cons to an action*

Case interviews often require you to make a recommendation to a hypothetical consulting client. Cost-benefit analysis is just another way of saying "weigh the pros and cons" of a decision before making a recommendation. For example, if your interviewer asks you to determine whether your client should close a plant, you can begin your answer by saying, "First I would look at the costs and benefits of this course of action," and then proceed to discuss them.

Internal vs. external market factors *Company's operations & external issues are the possible source*

This basic framework reminds you that a company's performance is affected both by its own actions and by external market factors. For example, let's say your interviewer asks you: "Our client is a major airline whose profits have fallen by half this year. Why?" You should discuss both the firm's own actions as possible causes for its drop in profits (for example, its expansion into new markets, marketing strategy, labor policies, etc.) as well as external market forces (for example, price-cutting by competitors, rising fuel prices, a tight labor market, etc.).

Fixed vs. variable costs → *rent, overhead no variation w/production vs variable cost for production*

There are two types of costs: fixed costs and variable costs. Fixed costs are those incurred by a company month after month regardless of what it does or how much it produces (for example, rent and overhead), so they do not vary with production levels. Variable costs, on the other hand, are expenses which rise or fall depending on the company's level of production. When making decisions in the short run, only variable costs should be considered since the company can't change its fixed costs in the short run. (Note: In the long run, nearly all costs are variable, even things like rent. For example, over the long run, the firm can move to smaller offices or even to another state or country with lower operating costs.)

A related concept is "sunk costs," or expenditures which have already been made and are not recoverable. Since sunk costs can't be recovered, they should not be factored into your decision-making. (Costs which are not yet spent or are recoverable are called "relevant costs.")

Hungry for more inside scoop? Join Vault.com's popular
online community for consulting — www.vault.com

VAULT.com   **27**

Opportunity cost

Every decision has an opportunity cost. This means simply that if you choose to do one thing, it may preclude doing something else. For example, if you stand in line for three hours to get a "free CD," you have in actuality "spent" on that CD whatever three hours of your time is worth. When analyzing a possible decision in a case interview, try to examine all possible opportunity costs that the subject of the case might incur by making or not making a particular decision.

Basic Accounting Concepts

Even if you're not an MBA, many consulting firms, especially those with strong financial consulting bents, will expect you to have some comprehension of basic accounting tools. If you haven't studied accounting, don't panic – these concepts are relatively easy to grasp. Here are some essential accounting tools.

Basic overview of financial statements

There are four basic financial statements that provide financial statement users with the information they need to evaluate a company. They include:

- The Balance Sheet
- The Income Statement
- The Statements of Retained Earning
- The Statements of Cash Flows

In addition, a company's annual report is almost always accompanied by notes to the financial statements. The notes to the financial statements provide additional information about the numbers provided in the four basic financial statements.

The next four sections provide a general overview of the four basic financial statements.

The Balance Sheet — Assets, Liabilities, Equity

The Balance Sheet presents the financial position of a company at a given point in time. It is comprised of three parts: Assets, Liabilities, and Equity. Assets are the economic resources of a company. They are the resources that the company uses to operate its business and include Cash, Inventory, and Equipment (accounts in financial statements are capitalized). A company normally obtains the resources it uses to operate its business by incurring debt, obtaining new investors, or through operating earnings. The Liabilities section of the Balance Sheet presents the debts of the company. Liabilities are the claims that creditors have on the company's resources. The Equity section of the Balance Sheet presents the net worth of a company, which equals the assets that the company owns less the debts they owe to creditors. Equity can also be defined as the claims that investors have on the company's resources.

$$Equity = Assets - Liabilities$$

Hungry for more inside scoop? Join Vault.com's popular
online community for consulting — www.vault.com

VAULT.com **29**

This example uses the basic format of a Balance Sheet:

Media Entertainment, Inc
Balance Sheet
December 31, 1998

Assets		Liabilities	
Cash		Accounts Payable	
203,000		7,000	
Accounts Receivable			
26,000		**Equity**	
Building		Common Stock	
19,000		10,000	
		Retained Earnings	
		231,000	
Total Assets		**Total Liabilities & Equity**	
248,000		248,000	

Because a company can obtain resources from both investors and creditors, one must be able to distinguish between the two and understand why one type is classified as a Liability and the other type is classified as Equity. Companies incur debt to obtain the economic resources necessary to operate their businesses and promise to pay the debt back over a specified period of time. This promise to pay is fixed and is not based upon the operating performance of the company. Companies also seek new investors to obtain economic resources. However, they don't promise to pay investors back a specified amount over a specified period of time. Instead, companies promise investors a return on their investment that is often contingent upon a certain level of operating performance. Since an equity holder's investment is not guaranteed, it is more risky in nature that a loan made by a creditor. But if a company performs well, the return to investors is often higher. The "promise-to-pay" element makes loans made by creditors a Liability and, as an accountant would say, more "senior" than equity holdings.

To summarize, the Balance Sheet represents the economic resources of a business, including the claims that creditors and equity holders have on those resources. Debts owed to creditors are more senior than the investments of equity holders and are classified as Liabilities, while equity investments are accounted for in the Equity section of the Balance Sheet.

The Income Statement

We have discussed two of the three ways in which a company normally obtains the economic resources necessary to operate its business: by incurring debt and by seeking new investors. A third way in which a company can obtain resources is through its own operations. The Income Statement presents the results of operations of a business over a specified period of time (e.g. one year, one quarter, one month) and is composed of Revenues, Expenses, and Net Income. Revenue is a source of income that normally arises from the sale of goods or services that the company is in business to sell and is recorded when it is earned. For example, when a retailer of roller blades makes a sale, the sale would be considered revenue. However, income may also come from other sources. For example, selling a business segment or a piece of capital equipment generates a type of revenue for a company. This type of income would be considered a Gain on Sale. Gains are sources of income from peripheral or incidental transactions (all economic events that are not usual and frequent).

Expenses: Expenses are the costs incurred by a business over a specified period of time to generate the revenues earned during that same period of time. For example, in order for a manufacturing company to sell a product, it must buy the materials it needs to make the product. In addition, that same company must pay people to both make and sell the product. The company must also pay salaries to the individuals who operate the business. These are all types of expenses that a company can incur during the normal operations of the business. When a company incurs an expense outside of its normal operations, it is considered a "loss." Losses are expenses incurred as a result of one-time or incidental transactions. The destruction of office equipment in a fire, for example, would be a loss.

Incurring expenses and acquiring assets both involve the use of economic resources (i.e. cash or debt). So when is a purchase considered an asset and when is it considered an expense?

ongoing return   • this period only

Assets vs. expenses: A purchase is considered an asset if it provides future economic benefit to the company, while expenses only relate to the current period. For example, monthly salaries paid to employees are for services that they already provided to the company during the month and would be considered expenses. On the other hand, the purchase of a piece of manufacturing equipment would be classified as an asset, as it will probably be used to manufacture a product for more than one accounting period.

Net income: The Revenue a company earns, less its Expenses during a specified period of time, equals its Net Income. A positive Net Income number indicates

Revenue - Expenses = net income

Hungry for more inside scoop? Join Vault.com's popular
online community for consulting — www.vault.com

VAULT.com   **31**

a profit, while a negative Net Income number indicates that a company suffered a loss (called a "net loss").

Here is an example of an Income Statement:

Media Entertainment, Inc
Income Statement
(For the year ended December 31, 1998)

Revenues		
Services Billed		100,000
Expenses		
Salaries and Wages	(33,000)	
Rent Expense	(17,000)	
Utilities Expense	(7,000)	(57,000)
Net Income		43,000

To summarize, the Income Statement measures the success of a company's operations; it provides investors and creditors with information to determine the profitability and creditworthiness of the enterprise. A company has earned net income when its total revenues exceed its total expenses. A company has a net loss when total expenses exceed total revenues.

The Statement of Retained Earnings

The Statement of Retained Earnings is a reconciliation of the Retained Earnings account from the beginning to the end of the year. When a company announces income or declares dividends, this information is reflected in the Statement of Retained Earnings. Net income increases the Retained Earnings account. Net losses and dividend payments decrease Retained Earnings.

Here is an example of a basic Statement of Retained Earnings:

Media Entertainment, Inc
Statement of Retained Earnings
(For the year ended December 31, 1998)

Retained Earnings, January 1, 1998	$200,000
Plus: Net income for the year	43,000
	243,000
Less: Dividends declared	(12,000)
Retained Earnings, December 31, 1998	$ 231,000

As you can probably tell by looking at this example, the Statement of Retained Earnings doesn't provide any new information not already reflected in other financial statements. But it does provide additional information about what management is doing with the company's earnings. Management may be "plowing back" the company's net income into the business by retaining part or all of its earnings, distributing its current income to shareholders, or distributing current and accumulated income to shareholders. (Investors can use this information to align their investment strategy with the strategy of a company's management. An investor interested in growth and returns on capital may be more inclined to invest in a company that "plows back" its resources into the company for the purpose of generating additional resources. Conversely, an investor interested in receiving current income is more inclined to invest in a company that pays quarterly dividend distributions to shareholders.)

The Statement of Cash Flows

Remember that the Income Statement provides information about the economic resources involved in the operation of a company. However, the Income Statement does not provide information about the actual source and use of cash generated during its operations. That's because obtaining and using economic resources doesn't always involve cash. For example, let's say you went shopping and bought a new mountain bike on your credit card in July – but didn't pay the bill until August. Although the store did not receive cash in July, the sale would still be considered July revenue. The statement of cash flows presents a detailed

Hungry for more inside scoop? Join Vault.com's popular
online community for consulting — www.vault.com

VAULT.com   33

summary of all of the cash inflows and outflows during the period and is divided into three sections based on three types of activity:

- Cash flows from operating activities: includes the cash effects of transactions involved in calculating net income

- Cash flows from investing activities: involves items classified as assets in the Balance Sheet and includes the purchase and sale of equipment and investments

- Cash flows from financing activities: involves items classified as liabilities and equity in the Balance Sheet; it includes the payment of dividends as well as issuing payment of debt or equity

Here is an example that shows the basic format of the Statement of Cash Flows:

Media Entertainment, Inc
Statement of Cash Flows
For the year ended December 31, 1998

Cash flows provided from operating activities		
Net Income	33,000	
Depreciation Expense	10,000	
Increase in Accounts Receivable	(26,000)	
Increase in Accounts Payable	7,000	(9,000)
Net cash provided by operating activities	24,000	
Cash flows provided from investing activities		
Purchase of Building	(19,000)	
Sale of Long-Term Investment	35,000	
Net cash provided by investing activities	16,000	
Cash flows provided from financing activities		
Payment of Dividends	(12,000)	
Issuance of Common Stock	10,000	
Net cash provided by financing activities	(2,000)	
Net increase (decrease) in cash	38,000	
Cash at the beginning of the year	165,000	
Cash at the end of the year	203,000	

As you can tell be looking at the above example, the Statement of Cash Flows gets its information from all three of the other financial statements:

• Net income from the Income Statement is shown in the section "cash flows from operating activities."

• Dividends from the Statement of Retained Earnings is shown in the section "cash flows from financing activities."

• Investments, Accounts Payable, and other asset and liability accounts from the Balance Sheet are shown in all three sections.

Hungry for more inside scoop? Join Vault.com's popular
online community for consulting — www.vault.com

VAULT.com   **35**

Advanced Concepts and Frameworks

MBAs and other candidates with business backgrounds, take note – interviewers will expect you to have a more detailed take on your case than an undergraduate would have. Here are some commonly used case concepts.

Net present value

Perhaps the most important type of decision company managers must make on a daily basis is whether to undertake a proposed investment. For example, should the company buy a certain piece of equipment? Build a particular factory? Invest in a new project? These types of decisions are called capital budgeting decisions. The consultant makes such decisions by calculating the net present value of each proposed investment and making only those investments that have positive net present values.

The net present value (or NPV) of an investment is simply the present value of the series of cash flows generated by the investment, minus the initial investment. The example on the following pages shows how to calculate NPV.

$$NPV = -C_0 + \frac{C_1}{(1+r)} + \frac{C_2}{(1+r)^2} + \frac{C_3}{(1+r)^3} +...+ \frac{C_t}{(1+r)^t}$$

Where: $C_0 =$ Initial Investment
$C_t =$ Cash flow in year t
$r =$ Discount rate

Example: *Hernandez is the CFO of Western Manufacturing Corp., an automobile manufacturer. The company is considering opening a new factory in Ohio that will require an initial investment of $1 million. The company forecasts that the factory will generate after-tax cash flows of $100,000 in Year 1, $200,000 in Year 2, $400,000 in Year 3, and $400,000 in Year 4. At the end of Year 4, the company would then sell the factory for $200,000. The company uses a discount rate of 12 percent. Hernandez must determine whether the company should go ahead and build the factory. To make this decision, Hernandez must calculate the net present value of the investment. The cash flows associated with the factory are as follows:*

Year 0	Year 1	Year 2	Year 3	Year 4
-$ 1,000,000	+ $100,000	+ $200,000	+ $400,000	+ $400,000
				+$200,000 (Sell Factory)
				+ $600,000

Hernandez then calculates the NPV of the factory as follows:

$$NPV = -\$1,000,000 + \frac{100,000}{1.12} + \frac{200,000}{(1.12)^2} + \frac{400,000}{(1.12)^3} + \frac{600,000}{(1.12)^4}$$

$$= -\$1,000,000 + \$89,286 + \$159,439 + \$284,712 + \$381,311$$

$$= -\$85,252$$

Since the factory has a negative net present value, Hernandez correctly decides that the factory should not be built.

The net present value rule

Note from the example above that once the consultant has figured out the NPV of a proposed investment, she then decides whether to undertake the investment by applying the net present value rule:

Make only those investments that have a positive net present value.

As long as the consultant follows this rule, she can be confident that each investment is making a positive net contribution to the company.

Hungry for more inside scoop? Join Vault.com's popular
online community for consulting — www.vault.com

VAULT.com **37**

The Capital Asset Pricing Model (CAPM)

In the above example, we assumed a given discount rate. However, part of a consultant's job is to determine an appropriate discount rate (r) to use when calculating net present values. The discount rate may vary depending on the investment.

Beta

The first step in arriving at an appropriate discount rate for a given investment is determining the investments riskiness. The market risk of an investment is measured by its "beta" (ß), which measures riskiness when compared to the market as a whole. An investment with a beta of 1 has the same riskiness as the market as a whole (so, for example, when the market moves down 10 percent, the value of the investment will on average fall 10 percent as well). An investment with beta of 2 will be twice as risky as the market (so when the market falls 10 percent, the value of the investment will on average fall 20 percent).

CAPM

Once the consultant has determined the beta of a proposed investment, he can use the Capital Asset Pricing Model (CAPM) to calculate the appropriate discount rate (r):

$$r = r_f + \beta(r_m - r_f)$$

$$\text{Where: } r = \text{discount rate}$$

$$r_f = \text{The risk-free rate of return}$$

$$r_m = \text{Market rate of return}$$

$$\beta = \text{Beta of the investment}$$

The risk-free rate of return is the return the company could receive by making a risk-free investment (for example, by investing in U.S. Treasury bills). The market rate of return is the return the company could receive by investing in a well-diversified portfolio of stocks (for example, S&P 500).

> *Example: Shen, Inc., a coal producer, is considering investing in a new venture that would manufacture and market carbon filters. Shen's chief financial officer, Apelbaum, wants to calculate the NPV of the proposed venture in order to determine*

whether the company should make the investment. After studying the riskiness of the proposed venture, Apelbaum determines that the beta of the investment is 1.5. A U.S. Treasury note of comparable maturity currently yields 7 percent, while the return on the S&P 500 stock index is 12 percent. Therefore, the discount rate Apelbaum will use when calculating the NPV of the investment will be:

$$r = .07 + 1.5\,(.12 - .07)$$
$$= .07 + .075$$
$$= .145$$
$$= 14.5\%$$

Although this is an overly simplified discussion of how consultants calculate discount rate to use in their cash-flow analysis, it does give you an overview of how consultants incorporate the notion of an investment's market to select the appropriate discount rate.

Hungry for more inside scoop? Join Vault.com's popular
online community for consulting — www.vault.com

VAULT.com **39**

Porter's Five Forces

Developed by Harvard Business School professor Michael Porter in his book *Competitive Strategy*, the Porter's Five Forces framework helps determine the attractiveness of an industry. Before any company expands into new markets, divests product lines, acquires new businesses, or sells divisions, it should ask itself, "Is the industry we're entering or exiting attractive?" By using Porter's Five Forces, a company can begin to develop a thoughtful answer. Consultants frequently utilize Porter's Five Forces as a starting point to help companies evaluate industry attractiveness.

Take, for example, entry into the copy store market (like Kinko's). How attractive is the copy store market?

Potential entrants: What is the threat of new entrants into the market? Copy stores are not very expensive to open – you can conceivably open a copy store with one copier and one employee. Therefore, barriers to entry are low, so there's a high risk of potential new entrants.

Buyer power: How much bargaining power do buyers have? Copy store customers are relatively price sensitive. Between the choice of a copy store that charges 5 cents a copy and a store that charges 6 cents a copy, buyers will usually head for the cheaper store. Because copy stores are common, buyers have the leverage to bargain with copy store owners on large print jobs, threatening to take their business elsewhere. The only mitigating factors are location and hours. On the other hand, price is not the only factor. Copy stores that are willing to stay open 24 hours may be able to charge a premium, and customers may simply patronize the copy store closest to them if other locations are relatively inconvenient.

Supplier power: How much bargaining power do suppliers have? While paper prices may be on the rise, copier prices continue to fall. The skill level employees need to operate a copy shop (for basic services, like copying, collating, etc.) are relatively low as well, meaning that employees will have little bargaining power. Suppliers in this situation have low bargaining power.

Threat of substitutes: What is the risk of substitution? For basic copying jobs, more people now possess color printers at home. Additionally, fax machines have the capability to fulfill copy functions as well. Large companies will normally have their own copying facilities. However, for large-scale projects, most individuals and employees at small companies will still use the services of a copy shop. The Internet is a potential threat to copy stores as well, because some documents that formerly would be distributed in hard copy will now be posted on the Web or sent through e-mail. However, for the time being, there is still relatively strong demand for copy store services.

Competition: Competition within the industry appears to be intense. Stores often compete on price, and are willing to "underbid" one another to win printing contracts. Stores continue to add new features to compete as well, such as expanding hours to 24-hour service and offering free delivery.

From this analysis, you can ascertain that copy stores are something of a commodity market. Consumers are very price-sensitive, copy stores are inexpensive to set up, and the market is relatively easily entered by competitors. Advances in technology may reduce the size of the copy store market. Value-added services, such as late hours, convenient locations, or additional services such as creating calendars or stickers, may help copy stores differentiate themselves. But overall, the copy store industry does not appear to be an attractive one.

As dot-coms come under fire, one case question we've heard increasingly is "How would you create barriers to entry as an Internet Startup?"

Hungry for more inside scoop? Join Vault.com's popular
online community for consulting — www.vault.com

VAULT.com   **41**

Product Life Cycle Curve

If you're considering a product case, figure out how "mature" your product or service is.

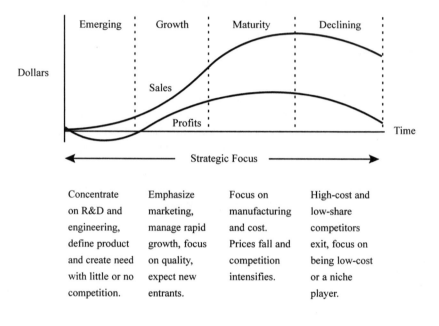

Product Life Cycle

Emerging	Growth	Maturity	Declining
Concentrate on R&D and engineering, define product and create need with little or no competition.	Emphasize marketing, manage rapid growth, focus on quality, expect new entrants.	Focus on manufacturing and cost. Prices fall and competition intensifies.	High-cost and low-share competitors exit, focus on being low-cost or a niche player.

Strategy tool/framework chart

Here's one way to think about the choice between being the lowest-cost provider or carving out a higher-end market niche – what consultants call differentiation.

Strategy	Low Cost	Differentiation
Required Capabilities	Efficient (large and dedicated) manufacturing facilities and lean overhead.	Ability to identify and deliver on non-priced-based purchase criteria (strong marketing, flexible manufacturing, etc.)
Typical Markets	Commodity, low-growth, or other markets with little brand awareness or differentiation	Markets where customers purchase based on non-price factors (quality, delivery, features, etc.)
Market Timing	Mature and declining markets	Emergent (grows out of preceding market), growth, and declining markets
Examples	Grain, gold, floppy disks, transportation, and temporary services	Breakfast cereal, formal attire, wine, and strategy consulting

Hungry for more inside scoop? Join Vault.com's popular
online community for consulting — www.vault.com

VAULT.com   **43**

The Four Ps

This is a useful framework for evaluating marketing cases. It can be applied to both products and services. The Four Ps consist of:

Price

The price a firm sets for its product/service can be a strategic advantage. For example, it can be predatory (set very low to undercut the competition), or it can be set slightly above market average to convey a "premium" image. Consider how pricing is being used in the context of the case presented to you.

Product

The product (or service) may provide strategic advantage if it is the only product/service that satisfies a particular intersection of customer needs. Or it may simply be an extension of already existing products, and therefore not much of a benefit. Try to tease out the value of the product in the marketplace based on the case details you have been given.

Position/Place

The physical location of a product/service can provide an advantage if it is superior to its competition, if it is easier or more convenient for people to consume, or if it makes the consumer more aware of the product/service over its competition. In the context of a business case, you may want to determine the placement of the product or service compared to its competition.

Promotion

With so much noise in today's consumer (and business to business) marketplace, it is difficult for any one product/service to stand out in a category. Promotional activity (including advertising, discounting to consumers and suppliers, celebrity appearances, etc.) can be used to create or maintain consumer awareness, open new markets, or target a specific competitor. You may want to suggest a promotional strategy in the context of the case you are presented relative to the promotional activity of other competing products/services.

The Four Cs

The Four Cs are especially useful for analyzing new product introductions and for industry analysis.

Customers

How is the market segmented?

What are the purchase criteria that customers use?

Competition

What is the market share of the clients?

What is its market position?

What is its strategy?

What is its cost position?

Does he/she have any market advantages?

Cost

What kind of economies of scale does the client have?

What is the client's experience curve?

Will increased production lower cost?

Capabilities

What resources can the client draw from?

How is the client organized?

What is the production system?

Hungry for more inside scoop? Join Vault.com's popular
online community for consulting — www.vault.com

VAULT.com   **45**

The Five Cs

This framework is mostly applied to financial cases and to companies (although it can be applied to individuals). You may employ it in other situations if you think it is appropriate.

Character

Evaluate the dedication, track record, and overall consumer perception of the company. Are there any legal actions pending against the company? If so, for what reason? Is the company progressive about its waste disposal, quality of life for its employees, and charitable contributions? What sort of impact would this have on the case you are evaluating?

Capacity

If you are dealing with a manufacturing entity, are its factories at, above, or below capacity, and for what reasons? Are there plans to add new plants, improve the technology in existing plants, or close underperforming plants? What about production overseas?

Capital

What is the company's cost of capital relative to its competitors? How healthy are its cash flows, revenues, and debt load relative to its competition?

Conditions

What is the current business climate the company (and its industry) faces? What is the short- and long-term growth potential in the industry? How is the market characterized? Is it emerging or mature? These questions can assist you in evaluating the facts of the case against the environment that the company/industry inhabits.

Competitive Advantage

This is the unique edge a company possesses over its competitors. It can be an unparalleled set of business processes, the ability to produce a product/service at a lower cost, charge a market premium, or any number of other assets that create an advantage over other market players. Whatever the case, these advantages are usually defensible and not easily copied.

In evaluating business cases using the Five Cs framework, you should look for those unique qualities that a company possesses and identify any that meet the criteria mentioned above. You may suggest that the company leverage its competitive advantage more aggressively or recommend alternatives if that company has no discernible advantage.

Value Chain Analysis

This approach involves assessing a company's overall business processes and identifying where that company actually adds value to a product or service. The total margin of profit will be the value of the product or service to buyers, less the cost of its production, as determined by the value chain.

In most cases, a competitive advantage is only temporary for many of today's products/services. Being first to market, having a unique formula or configuration, or having exclusivity in a market were once long-term defensible strategies. But today, businesses are globally connected by lightning-fast communications and knowledge-sharing systems and manufacturing technologies are getting better and faster at reacting to and anticipating market conditions. Thus these advantages are only fleeting or may not exist at all.

Value Chain Analysis attempts to identify a competitive advantage by deconstructing the various "changes" a company's business processes perform on a set of raw materials or other inputs. Most can be easily copied by other competitors, but there is usually a unique subset that represents the "value-added" qualities only the company under scrutiny possesses. This set is that company's competitive advantage, or "value chain." Sometimes this set can be copied, but a unique set of circumstances may still allow the company in question to perform them at a lower cost, charge a premium in the market, or retain higher market share than its competitors.

In the context of a business case, you can use this framework to identify a company's overall business processes set and then determine if one or more of the processes are defensible competitive advantages.

For example, a manufacturer of fruit juice might have the following value chain elements:

- Research and development (Will mango really taste good with cloudberry juice?)

- Cost of goods sold (How much does it cost to manufacture the fruit juice? Is there a frost in Florida that drives up the costs of oranges? Is the currency crisis in Indonesia making papaya very cheap? Are per-volume purchases lower than, for example, those of Tropicana?)

- Packaging and shipping (How much does that new banana-shaped container cost? Are many bottles lost in transit? What are the fixed costs of shipping?)

- Manufacturing (How much do those juice pulpers cost? How often do factories need to be reengineered?)

Hungry for more inside scoop? Join Vault.com's popular
online community for consulting — www.vault.com

VAULT.com   **47**

- Labor (How many employees do we have? Where are they located? Are they unionized?)

- Distribution (Where are the distribution centers? Where are the products distributed?)

- Advertising (Billboards, TV, magazines?)

- Margin (How profitable is the juice company?)

For more detailed information on this type of analysis, you may want to consider the authoritative text on competitive strategy: *Competitive Strategy: Techniques for Analyzing Industries and Competitors*, by Michael E. Porter.

Core competencies

"Core competencies" is the idea that each firm has a limited number of things it is very good at (that is, its core competence or competencies).

When restructuring or reengineering, one of the starting points for a company should be identifying its core competencies. A firm should define its core competencies broadly in order to be flexible enough to adapt to changes in the marketplace. (For instance, when Xerox defined itself as a "document company," rather than a maker of copy machines, it was able to take advantage of the more lucrative business of document handling and outsourcing for major corporations, as well as of the market for fax machines, scanners, and other document-handling equipment.)

Companies should seriously consider selling/spinning off business units that are not part of their "core" business. For instance, Pepsi recently spun off its restaurant operations after it concluded that its expertise was in manufacturing and marketing beverages, not in managing restaurants.

Benchmarking and "best practices"

A commonly used concept in consulting (especially in operations and implementation engagements) is "benchmarking." Benchmarking basically means researching what other companies in the industry are doing (usually in order to evaluate whether your client is operating efficiently or to identify areas where the client can cut costs). For example, if a mail-order company wants to reduce its order-processing costs, it would want to compare its order processing costs with those of other mail-order companies, breaking down its costs for each part of the process (including order-taking and shipping) and comparing them with industry averages. It can then pinpoint those areas where its costs are higher than average for the industry.

A related concept is "best practices": once you've benchmarked what other companies are doing, you want to focus on those companies that have particular low costs or which otherwise operate particularly well. What are they doing right (i.e., what are their "best practices")? And how can our client (in the case) emulate or copy what they're doing? Remember to look outside your client's particular industry, if necessary, to find the best practices for a particular process or operation.

The 2x2 matrix

The 2x2 matrix is a good framework to use any time you have two factors that, when combined, yield different outcomes. A very rudimentary example would be what happens when you turn on your bathroom faucets, as follows:

A more business-appropriate example would involve acquiring a company. Let's say a company is interested in understanding the difficulty of acquiring or building a distribution center and it is considering financing this decision with either stock or debt. The potential outcomes might look like this:

Hungry for more inside scoop? Join Vault.com's popular
online community for consulting — www.vault.com

VAULT.com **49**

The BCG Matrix

The BCG Matrix, named after the Boston Consulting Group (BCG), is perhaps the most famous 2x2 matrix. The matrix measures a company's relative market share on the horizontal axis and its growth rate on the vertical axis.

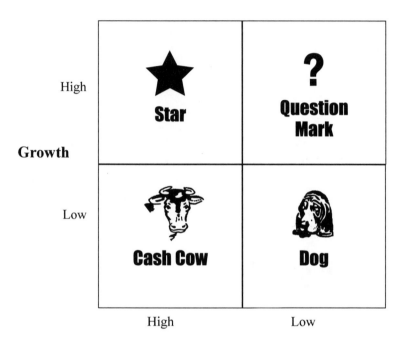

Relative Market Share (RMS)

M&A cases: Determining the drivers of value for an acquisition

Case interviews aren't just for consultants. Mergers & acquisition cases are wildly popular at investment banks. Here's how to analyze a potential acquisition.

Value Drivers (M&A) Framework

In order to understand value, we need to understand the three primary value drivers:

The value components can be further broken out into specific "value drivers":

Hungry for more inside scoop? Join Vault.com's popular
online community for consulting — www.vault.com

VAULT.com   **51**

Target & Market Assessment

The ultimate objective of a target & market assessment is to determine the value of the target.

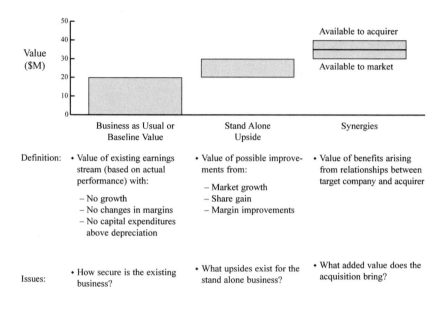

	Business as Usual or Baseline Value	Stand Alone Upside	Synergies

Definition:	• Value of existing earnings stream (based on actual performance) with:
	  – No growth
	  – No changes in margins
	  – No capital expenditures above depreciation
		• Value of possible improvements from:
		  – Market growth
		  – Share gain
		  – Margin improvements
			• Value of benefits arising from relationships between target company and acquirer

Issues:	• How secure is the existing business?	• What upsides exist for the stand alone business?	• What added value does the acquisition bring?

In assessing the factors driving value we can determine the outlook for the target itself, as well as the market in which it competes (see next page).

Market	**Target**

- Revenues

• What drives demand?	• Why do customers buy the target's products versus those of competitors?
• Is demand increasing?	
• What substitute products are available?	• Will the target's market share increase or decrease?
• What is the outlook for prices, given supply/demand and competitive rivalry?	• What price premium or discount does the target command?
• What is the regulatory environment?	• Is the target's market position sustainable?
	• What is the target's strength in supply chain?

- Costs

• Are industry costs increasing or decreasing?	• How is the target positioned versus competitor's costs?
• Is the industry becoming increasingly competitive?	• How is the target's cost position likely to change in the future?
• Is a technology shift likely?	

- Capital

• Is the business changing in a way that will require higher fixed or working capital in the future?	• How old is the target's plant?
	• What is its capacity?
	• What capital expenditures are needed for upgrades or expansion?
	• Is the target's working capital likely to change?

↓ | ↓

Is this an attractive business? | Is the target well positioned in this market?

Hungry for more inside scoop? Join Vault.com's popular
online community for consulting — www.vault.com

VAULT.com   **53**

M&A Cases: Data gathering and analysis

Market Analysis Tools

• Competitive position framework

• Relative value versus competitors to customer through supply chain

• Product life cycle

• Supply and demand analysis

    – Industry capacity

    – Industry utilization

    – Demand drivers

    – Regressions

• Segmentation analysis

• Porter's Five Forces

• Experience curves

• Trends and outlook

• Key success factors

Target Analysis Tools

• Business system – comparison with competitors

• Market share (over time and by segment)

• Capacity (growth and utilization of)

• Customer's key purchase criteria and relative performance

• Financial history

• Sales and profitability by segment

• Cash flow analysis

• Margin and expense structure

• Relative cost position

• Cost benchmarking

Your data gathering strategy will vary depending on industry:

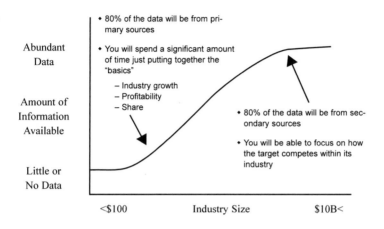

A framework caution

All the frameworks detailed above are widely used, and most U.S. business schools teach them as part of their core curriculums. Your interviewers will instantly recognize when you are applying them, since they are already familiar with the techniques. While this is OK, consider that you are trying to demonstrate your unique analytical and deductive reasoning skills that set you apart from other candidates. You must be creative and original in analyzing case questions. Use these frameworks sparingly. (Another note: No interviewer will be impressed if you proudly proclaim, "I'm going to apply Porter's Five Forces now." Apply frameworks without identifying them.)

Hungry for more inside scoop? Join Vault.com's popular
online community for consulting — www.vault.com

VAULT.com   **55**

BEING THERE

What it's like being in a case interview

Let's just pretend for a minute that you're Jane Candidate, and you have an interview at Boom Consulting. What might it be like? Here's what a sample 30-minute case interview might be like.

You are Jane Candidate. It's your first interview with a consulting firm. You're carefully dressed in your best navy suit (OK, so it's your roommate's best navy suit), you've charged a leather portfolio on your Visa card, and you've dutifully tucked a copy of your resume and transcript inside that glove-leather portfolio. It's time for your interview. You understand that these interviews last about half an hour.

You walk in, and are greeted by Jim Interviewer, who doesn't look much older than you. In fact, you vaguely remember him from the recruitment meeting you went to in October. You shake hands firmly.

"Hi, Jane," Jim says. "It's great to meet you. Everyone on the committee was very impressed by your resume." He sounds sincere.

"I'm glad to hear it," you say, hoping you look poised and confident.

"I'm an alum of Top Ten U. myself," says Jim. "What dorm do you live in?"

"Blank House," you tell him. "How about yourself?"

After a minute of chat about the Top Ten Pumas, Jim pulls out your resume (though you stashed a copy in your portfolio, just in case), and glances over it.

"I see you're the managing editor of the Top Ten Tribune," Jim says. "What was your toughest challenge as an editor?"

You talk about the Top Ten Tribune for a few minutes, talking about assignments you've given and the role of the newspaper at the university. At 10 after the hour, Jim looks at his watch and says, "I want to give you as much time as possible for the case. So unless you have any questions for me, let's get started."

You sit back and take a deep breath. Your case interview is about to begin!

The case

"Recently," says Jim, "I was at a strategy meeting with a consumer brand company. They told me that in the past two quarters, sales of their waffles had risen significantly."

"Their waffles?" you interject. "I don't know a lot about breakfast food marketing, but that doesn't seem like a product that would suddenly experience a big jump in sales."

"That's right, Jane," says Jim. "That's why they asked us to look into the matter. What would you do?"

Fortunately, you've done your research on how to structure cases. You think the Four P model might be a good way to structure this particular case. The Four Ps, you recall (without looking at your note pad), are price, position, promotion and product.

You tell Jim how you're going to proceed with your analysis.

"Let's break down the situation like this. First, I'm going to try to find out about the market position of the waffles. Then, I'm going to try to figure out how the waffles are being promoted. After that, I'll ask whether there are any price-based reasons for the surge in waffle sales. Finally, I'll ask you about the waffles themselves."

"That seems like a reasonable way to proceed," comments Jim.

"Okay, then," you say. "What is the overall market for waffles? Has it grown recently?"

"No," says Jim. "Demand for waffles seems to be holding steady."

"That means we're taking our waffle sales from other waffle manufacturers."

"It seems so," confirms Jim.

"Is there a seasonal reason for this increase in waffle consumption? Perhaps people eat more waffles when it's cold?"

"No, our waffles sales are normally steady year-round."

"Have sales of other breakfast foods, or our own breakfast products, increased as well?"

"No, they haven't," says Jim. "There seems to be no uptick in the breakfast food market."

Hungry for more inside scoop? Join Vault.com's popular
online community for consulting — www.vault.com

VAULT.com **59**

"Has our client entered any new markets recently? Perhaps they've entered the Asian market? I'm assuming that these waffles are only sold in North American markets."

"Your assumption is correct, and that is a good question," says Jim. "In fact, the company does plan to expand into the European and Asian markets. That's why they want to know the reason behind the sales upsurge – so they can replicate it. But for the time being, no, they haven't expanded the sales area."

You're getting a little frustrated, but so far, Jim hasn't indicated that your reasoning is unsound.

"Okay, let's talk about promotion and price," you say. "Has our client lowered prices recently?"

"No," says Jim.

"Have other waffle manufacturers raised their prices?"

"Nope," says Jim.

"Is our product a premium product – have we raised prices?"

"No," says Jim. "There is little price differential between our waffles and competing waffle products. And prices have not varied in the past two quarters. In fact, our waffles are slightly more expensive than some waffles, and a bit less than others."

You get the feeling that Jim is telling you to back off the price issue.

"Then maybe there's some kind of promotion going on. Has the company started advertising its waffles? Is it promoting a related product, like syrup?"

Jim answers no to both.

"Maybe the price of all syrup has gone down?" you guess.

"That would affect the consumption of all waffles," says Jim.

You guess blindly: "Is there a celebrity who's recently become famous for eating our waffles?"

Jim laughs. "That's not it."

"Then tell me about our client's promotion process," you say.

"Our client spends about $10 million yearly on waffle promotion. Every month, we run advertisements in three selected magazines. We also have coupon promotions and a commercial that runs on TV."

Now, you think, you're on to something! "Have we started to put our commercials on more popular programs? Has the quality of our advertising improved?"

To your frustration, Jim shakes his head. "We haven't significantly changed our promotion campaign. The ratings of the shows we advertise on are about the same. We have noticed more use of our coupons, however."

"Has the demographic of our advertising changed?" you ask. "Is the client now pitching to people who are more likely to eat waffles?"

"As far as we can tell, the makeup and audience of our advertising hasn't changed," says Jim.

You're determined to uncover the reason behind this waffle case – and you don't have that much time left. "Then perhaps something has changed about our product," you say. "Has the shape changed?"

"Well," says Jim, "it has changed a bit."

"How so?"

"It's flattened out somewhat."

"Why? Has the production process changed?"

"Yes, it has," says Jim. "We're using a new template for the waffles as part of a general factory modernization."

"Are the ingredients the same?"

"Those have changed too. We're using a new supplier."

"Then," you say, "I would venture to guess that consumers in North America prefer a flatter, larger waffle. There must be something about the new production process that has created a better waffle."

"Yes," says Jim. "Our focus groups show that the texture and crispiness of the waffle has improved. Consumers are responding to our inadvertently improved waffle."

"Then I recommend that we investigate whether European and Asian markets would respond in a similar manner to our new waffle product. We should also promote our waffle advantage in the market. Perhaps we could enter new markets for waffles, like using them for dinner, as crepes."

"Your suggestions are interesting and we'll look at them later," says Jim. "Good job! Do you have any questions for me about Boom Consulting?"

Hungry for more inside scoop? Join Vault.com's popular
online community for consulting — www.vault.com

VAULT.com   **61**

REAL LIFE
INTERVIEWS

There's no substitute for experience. Read on for some from-the-trenches accounts of real-life consulting interviews. Please keep in mind that these are the unique experiences of individuals and should not be construed as the typical case experience in any consulting firm. Consulting interviews may vary by office and interviewer.

Boston Consulting Group, MBA

I had five case interviews at BCG and two regular interviews. What was unusual was that two different people asked me to look at data and charts and talk about what was said, as opposed to talking about a case per se. That's a typically unusual BCG thing to do. They'd show you, for example, a data table and a graph.

One of my cases was about a content syndication company, and one was about a paper company that was becoming less profitable. (Apparently a lot of cases are about paper companies, because they're big business but no one knows anything about them offhand.) You should think about revenue and fixed versus variable costs.

Sometimes cases are not set in the present day. I had one case set in 1985 specifically so I couldn't offer Internet solutions.

Another case was about a pharmaceutical company trying to go online. The case asked what the best way would be to determine which services you put online and which you wouldn't. You have to think about who the customers were and the supply chain — basically, the 4 Ps.

I found BCG consultants to be friendly — my interviews were more like discussions. In one instance, I had trouble with a data chart. I asked for help and got good hints. I suggest that you stop in the beginning of the BCG case and take notes or you will get lost. The case is usually 20 to 25 minutes.

McKinsey, MBA

I had six case interviews with McKinsey. I had a few interviewers who I didn't feel were very nice — they seemed to want you to get the case wrong.

I found, and it was the experience of my fellow MBA students interviewing as well, that the cases at McKinsey are very quantitative. A lot of cases at McKinsey were about estimating market size and there is sometimes difficult math. I struggled a little bit with some of the calculations and they would throw something in to speed things up, like "Oh, why don't we just say 20 million." On the other hand, I had one interview where I had two market sizings, and you were only supposed to have one. I solved it too fast, so I got another one.

I had to estimate the size of the restaurant market in New York City and estimate the number of cars produced on an assembly line every day. That was complicated. I had to calculate how quickly the conveyor belt was moving, the schedule of the factory, etc. Sometimes they would add new information, like "Let's say the factory is closed on Sunday."

I also had a few others. Here was one case: You have five million dollars. You can buy a building in New York City or you can invest it at 7 percent return. It's a discounted cash flow problem. You had to determine what kind of building it was, what kind of location, what the income was from rental, estimate the volatility of the real estate market.

I also had the question "What will your phone bill look like in five years?"

Keep in mind that you're being watched every minute you're in the office. I know some people who discussed their cases while they were in the bathroom. They didn't get an offer.

Hungry for more inside scoop? Join Vault.com's popular
online community for consulting — www.vault.com

V/\ULT.com   **65**

Monitor, undergraduate

Monitor has a weird case process. They have a written case they give you with a lot of data and numbers. There are four specific questions you have to answer, some of them quantitative. They do allow you to have a calculator. Afterwards you talk through your answers. Mine was a manufacturer, its market size, its main competitors, and how it should increase their revenues. They use the same case for everyone on the same day, I hear.

The final round is a group interview. You get data and are asked to pull qualitative data out. You have half an hour to look at the problem and develop a quick presentation to the whole group. Then you talk about the presentation together, like you were an engagement team. Everyone was pretty cautious. They didn't know whether or not to be aggressive. In general, everyone was friendly or supportive. Afterwards they show you a staged presentation of a client-consultant situation and ask you for your feedback and what you would have done in the same situation.

Arthur Andersen, undergraduate

For me, the first round was all behavioral. They asked about your behavior in certain circumstances. I did find it odd because they seemed to want you to talk the entire interview. The other companies interacted with you more. They wanted you to talk about your experiences. In the second round they have a presentation case, which you work through and then present to a panel.

Hungry for more inside scoop? Join Vault.com's popular
online community for consulting — www.vault.com

VAULT.com   **67**

A.T. Kearney, undergraduate

My experience was atypical. [A.T. Kearney] doesn't have a lot of people at the undergraduate level and they are very top-heavy. They describe it to me as an inverted pyramid. At the first interview, I didn't have a case. I was asked about where I saw A.T. Kearney fitting into the consulting scheme of things. They are very interested in differentiating themselves. I had one interview where I was given a lot of information that essentially said that Internet companies were all overvalued and that to justify their valuations a virtually impossible number of people would need to get online. Then she asked me what I thought. I think she just wanted to see how much I knew about the Internet economy.

I had one case with a manufacturer of computer products. I had to figure out how to save them ten million dollars. After asking a lot of questions, the key takeaway was that they had a lot of computers on the shelf. They needed to speed up the manufacturing and shipping process. That's because computers lose value very quickly.

I had another interview that was also about computer manufacturers. It was about a company trying to get into selling services. I had to identify key points for the business plan.

L.E.K., MBA

I had two cases in the first round. One was fit and the second one was a case interview. The interview just looked at me and said, "I've been thinking a lot about the Web boxes on televisions. What are some of your thoughts about their viability?" They really wanted to see if you knew anything about the tech market. I would recommend reading the *Industry Standard* before interviewing with L.E.K. because they are all about the Internet.

In my second case, I was given a lot of different scenarios about a generic sort of company and we had to draw a lot of graphs. They would say things like, "We have a cost structure where it's variable up until a certain point but after that it's fixed, and we have these costs. Okay, what if you took out variable costs?" It was all about the line graph.

They don't pay for any interview expenses until the final round.

In the second round, I met with managers [senior consultants]. I had a neat case about the Internet. It was thinking about the advantages and disadvantages of moving operations online if you're a bricks-and-mortar retailer. They wanted to make sure that I understood current events about technology and that the Internet company isn't always linked with the parent company. We talked about Nordstrom.com for a while.

The second half of the interview, I was asked to explain anything I was passionate about.

I was also asked a lot of questions about Excel, and the most advanced thing I had done on Excel, which I found odd.

Hungry for more inside scoop? Join Vault.com's popular
online community for consulting — www.vault.com

V/\ULT.com   **69**

BUSINESS CASES

Following is a sampling of business case questions. Some are provided with suggested answers or lines of reasoning. Remember that there is no right answer to these questions, so what follows each question is a suggested outline or framework for working through your solution. You may use any line of reasoning you are comfortable with, but remember to be concise and confident, and to make NO assumptions. If you don't have enough facts to move forward, ask! Only if your interviewer refuses to give you information should you make sensible assumptions – while informing the interviewer that you're making them. Sketching out a few graphs may help clarify your analysis (and impress your interviewer, as graphs are the coin of the consulting trade). Increasingly, interviewers may ask you to interpret data or graphs as part of your case.

PRACTICE QUESTIONS

1 ## Leaving on a Jet Plane

A major airline is considering the purchase of 24 new planes. They are unclear how this purchase will affect their business performance in the short term as well as the long term. You are the Senior Consultant meeting with the Operating Committee for the first time. I am the Chief Operating Officer of the company. What would you need to know from me in order to assess the situation?

Here is a good example of a directed question combined with a role-playing exercise. Not only will the interviewer be assessing your analysis and deductive abilities, but she will also be evaluating your poise and professionalism in front of a senior executive. In many cases, consultants find themselves in front of key client personnel who are older and more experienced in the industry, so your ability to cope with this type of situation is essential. How will you actually go about assessing the situation and finding information once you arrive at the client? (This case was given to an MBA-level candidate.)

You: What is the planned delivery cycle of the new aircraft? Will it be staggered, serial, or all at once?

Interviewer: Aircraft will be delivered as they are manufactured over the next five years, at approximately four per year.

You: How many planes are in the current fleet? Are there any plans to sell off older aircraft as the newer aircraft are delivered?

Interviewer: There are 120 planes in the current fleet. There are no plans to get rid of our older aircraft as the new ones arrive.

You: What is the current average cost per flight-hour of the fleet?

Interviewer: It varies by aircraft type. The range is anywhere from $1,000 to $5,000.

You: Do you have any frameworks in mind for assessing this situation?

Interviewer: No, what would you suggest? (This is a tough response because it asks you to put a stake in the ground.)

Hungry for more inside scoop? Join Vault.com's popular
online community for consulting — www.vault.com

VAULT.com   **73**

You: Well, in many cases I have used a company's cost of capital, relative to the average cost of capital in the industry, industry-specific metrics like the cost per flight-hour, as I already mentioned, and depreciation method choice. I would also want to assess the new efficiencies brought about by your purchase, as in fuel cost savings, increased passenger load, and so on. Do these sound reasonable to you?

Interviewer: Yes, as a beginning. How will you go about finding the information you need?

You: I would first need to know appropriate contact people in purchasing, finance, and accounting who could provide the quantitative facts I need to perform the assessment. With your introduction, I would like to meet with each of these people from two hours to a half-day in order to gather the information. I would need to circle back through each of them after the initial interviews simply to validate the information I have compiled, once I have assembled a draft.

Interviewer: That sounds like a workable plan.

2 | Help! Our Profit Margins are Shrinking!

You are the consultant to a company that produces large household appliances. Over the past three years, profit margins have fallen 20 percent and market share has tumbled to 15 percent of the market from 25 percent. What is the source of the company's problems?

This is an example of the type of question an undergraduate student (or an MBA student in an early interview round) might receive. The interviewer has done you the favor of defining the problem – your client is in something of a slump! This dialogue illustrates how you, the perspicacious candidate, might drill down into the core of the woes besetting the firm.

You: How would you characterize the current marketplace for these products? Emerging? Mature?

Interviewer: The product line is considered mature.

You: How would you characterize your manufacturing process relative to your competition? (You're looking to see if the company has a strategic advantage.)

Interviewer: Can you be more specific?

You: Do you benefit from an advantage in technology, economies of scale, exchange rates, or other manufacturing element over your competition?

Interviewer: We have not updated our manufacturing process since 1988. We manufacture our products exclusively in the United States. As one of the oldest manufacturers of these products, we have a reliable customer base and a good reputation. As for price, we are one of the lower-priced in the market, though not the lowest.

You: Do any of your competitors manufacture overseas?

Interviewer: Our number one competitor produces all of its appliances in Indonesia. (Here's your clue – manufacturing outside the country significantly lowers costs.)

You: It probably suffices to say that some of your decline in profit can be attributed to the increased costs you are facing relative to older manufacturing techniques and higher costs associated with manufacturing domestically. This is especially toxic in a mature market where consumers are mostly aware of the product

Hungry for more inside scoop? Join Vault.com's popular
online community for consulting — www.vault.com

VAULT.com **75**

category and the product may be considered a commodity. (A commodity marketplace is one in which customers make their purchasing decisions largely on price. For example, toilet paper is largely a commodity market, where consumers buy whatever's on sale.)

Let's talk about market share now. Can you tell me about any recent market research you have regarding the strength of your brand, price, your products' position, and any promotional activity you have had?

Interviewer: Our market research department has told us that consumers are confused about the product category, that they do not understand the differences between our brand and our competitors' brands. We sell to all major appliance retailers in the U.S. We promote aggressively twice a year, and have smaller promotions once a quarter. (This is consistent with the description of a commodity product. The ways of breaking out of commodity markets include promotions and making value-added differences in the brand – like, in the case of toilet paper, introducing new designer colors and specially quilted cotton-blend paper.)

You: What form does your promotional activity take?

Interviewer: We offer a price discount to consumers twice a year. We regularly advertise in major magazines targeted to our consumer, and we have an active outdoor campaign underway.

You: It would appear you are competing in an undifferentiated marketplace and there may be an opportunity to capture additional share through an aggressive brand differentiation effort. I believe it would also be worth investigating the efficacy of your current promotional programs, relative to your competition. The consumer may be responsive to other types of promotions that haven't been utilized by the company as of yet.

3

Banking on Savings

A bank is trying to increase its operating efficiency. Your consulting team has been asked to look at the non-interest, non-personnel expense base in order to cut costs. How would you determine the potential size of the opportunity for operating efficiency? What issues might arise in such a study?

This is an exercise in full-value procurement (FVP). FVP is a rationalization across business units of common purchases and services. The measure of an FVP is the amount of "spend" reduced, defined as the cost savings realized by reducing the number of sources from which common products/services are purchased. (This question, and questions like it that require advanced frameworks, are much more likely to be received by business school candidates and case interviewees with significant business experience than by undergraduates with no business experience.)

In this case interview, your interviewer will impersonate the client. Case interviews often take this kind of role-playing form (which can be fun!).

You: What is your revenue level on an annual basis like?

Interviewer: In 1998 our revenues were $1.2 billion. (These seem to be the revenues of a prosperous regional bank, not a bulge bracket.)

You: What are the common items and services that all business units use? Do you have common office suppliers or housekeeping services?

Interviewer: Well, obviously we have most common office products shared across all our functions. We also have cleaning services for our corporate headquarters, our printing center, and our retail locations.

You: How many vendors provide similar products and services to the bank?

Interviewer: We buy office products from OfficeMax's corporate services in Indiana, Avery Dennison corporate services in California, and someone else, the name of which escapes me right now, for the retail banks. Also, I believe we contract regionally for housekeeping services.

Hungry for more inside scoop? Join Vault.com's popular
online community for consulting — www.vault.com

VAULT.com   **77**

You: Is consolidating branch offices or reducing ATM counts a possibility?

Interviewer: Not at this time. In fact, we're planning to expand in three different states.

You: Are your cost concerns the result of an impending merger? (Perhaps the interviewer has deliberately left out an important piece of information – the bank has undergone, or is planning, a merger or acquisition of another bank that might drive up costs.)

Interviewer: No, our growth is organic, not through acquisition. (Looks like this is a dead end. Time to move on to other considerations.)

You: Have you considered outsourcing non-critical business tasks?

Interviewer: What kind do you suggest? (Your interviewer is probing to see if you can name the kind of services a bank might successfully outsource.)

You: Well, what about information systems, call centers and customers service, bill collection, document handling, those kind of things?

Interviewer: Oh, no. That's not possible. (Remember that this is a role play. This seems a bit uncommunicative for a reasonable suggestion; you should probe a bit further. Businesses aren't always entirely reasonable in their actions!)

You: Can you explain your objections?

Interviewer: Don't you think outsourcing those processes is extreme? We're a bank, and we have a lot of confidential information on both paper and electronic media. Our integrity would be put at risk if we let others manage our internal functions.

You: Well, sir, I understand your objections. However, many major corporations use organizations that centralize activities like copy centers and conference planning, all of which also have trade secrets and confidential information.

Interviewer: That sounds interesting, and I'd like more information. (Your interviewer graciously acknowledges the wisdom of your suggestions.) But can you give me a concrete suggestion my supervisor will like?

You: (Time to return to a less controversial aspect.) What would you estimate your spending to be for things like office products?

Interviewer: I estimate about $100 million on office products, corporation wide, in 1998, though you'd have to talk to our operations people, of course.

You: I think, based on your information, that there are ample opportunities for cost savings that I can identify right now. Reducing your vendors down to one or two will allow you to use economies of scale to extract cost savings. Outsourcing promises even greater savings.

Hungry for more inside scoop? Join Vault.com's popular
online community for consulting — www.vault.com

VAULT.COM   **79**

4   Paper or Air

> A restaurant owner is currently setting up a new restaurant and
> making some basic decisions on how to fit it out. He is today making a
> decision on the facilities to place in the restrooms for customers to dry
> their hands. Initial research suggests that he has three options – paper
> towels, roller towels and hot air dryers. What should he consider in his
> decision-making process?

In the initial analysis, you might ask a number of questions, which will influence
your decision.

- What type of restaurant is it going to be – luxurious, budget, middle-market?

- How many customers does he expect? (How many tables? Is it open during
  the day? In the evening?)

- Has he done any customer research to see what customers would prefer?

Fairly soon in the process, you should start asking questions about the economics
of the three options – in which case the interviewer will give you some more
information:

In the initial research, the restaurant owner has found out the following
information from the suppliers of the drying facilities:

- Dryers have an initial cost of $500 each (but you'll need two – one for each
  restroom) and monthly service charge of $100 per month. The supplier
  estimates that the lifetime of a dryer is four years.

- Paper towels cost 5 cents each and the number of paper towels that you will
  need (varies directly) with the number of customers. So if you expect 50
  customers a night, they will use 50 towels.

- If you use toweling rolls, they will cost $5 per roll (and again you'll need
  two – one for each restroom). The rolls will be changed daily if the
  restaurant has more than 2,000 customers per month or every other day if
  there are less than 2,000 customers per month.

At this point, it's obvious that from an economic standpoint, the option you select
will vary with the number of customers. Therefore, it makes sense to look at a
break-even calculation.

First of all, take the dryers. They cost $100 per month, plus an upfront charge of $1,000 that you should depreciate over their lifetime (i.e. an additional $1,000/(4 x 12) per month = $21 per month). Therefore their total cost is approximately $120 per month – and this does not vary with the number of customers coming into the restaurant.

Secondly, look at the paper towels option. These vary directly with the number of customers in the restaurant, at a cost of $0.05 per customer. Therefore with a low number of customers per month, paper towels will be cheaper than dryers will. How many customers would have to come to the restaurant each month to make the dryers more cost effective? The cost of towels would have to exceed $120 per month, equating to $120/$0.05 = 2,400 customers per month.

Is this break-even affected by the rolls option? At less than 2,000 customers per month, the rolls would cost $10 every other day or $10 x 15 days = $150 per month. This in itself is more costly than both the dryer and the towels option, and with more than 2,000 customers, it will only look more unfavorable.

Therefore the real economic decision is between towels and dryers. At less than 2,400 customers per month (or 2,400/30 = 80 customers per night) you would prefer the towels. Once the number of customers increases above this, you'd switch to the dryers' option.

Following the economic analysis, you might mention a few more non-economic points that might sway the balance:

- Are there additional staff costs of cleaning up paper towel waste?

- How many suppliers of each option are there? If there is a single supplier, might he have the capacity to raise prices in the future?

Hints on quantitative cases:

- Make the numbers easy – round up or down when possible to make further calculations easier.

- When you're jotting down numbers, make sure you keep a track of what is what, so when you pull together your recommendations at the end of the analysis, you can make comparisons between the options.

- In break-even cases, it is sometimes effective to draw a graph to illustrate the break-even decision (in this case, number of customers per month along the x-axis vs. cost of drying option along the y-axis).

Hungry for more inside scoop? Join Vault.com's popular
online community for consulting — www.vault.com

VAULT.COM **81**

5   Making a Case out of Lemons

Your niece approaches you and says "Since you're a management consultant, maybe you can help me. I want to buy my mother a present for her birthday, and I was thinking of opening a lemonade stand to earn the money. Tell me what you think of my plan."

Isn't she cute? Yet this is a serious case (from Bain, no less). The interviewer is trying to see if you can set up a value chain for your niece. Get out your notepad.

You: What kind of present do you want to get for your mother?

Interviewer: I want to get her a pair of gold earrings.

You: That's a very nice idea. I'm going to assume that you want to buy a pair of earrings that cost $50.

Interviewer: Actually, the earrings I want cost $100. (The interviewer is trying to raise the bar a bit.)

You: Okay. When is your mom's birthday? What's your time-frame?

Interviewer: My mother's birthday is in three months.

You: What kind of time commitment can you make to the lemonade stand? How many days a week do you plan to run the stand?

Interviewer: I have to go to school during the week, so I think just on weekends.

You: Here are some of the considerations you need to make if you want to earn $100 in three months from your lemonade stand.

     What are your expenses? Let's say that you need to buy the pitcher, which is $2. Every 100 plastic cups will cost you $1 in direct costs. Those are your base expenses.

     You then have to make several cost decisions. What size cups will you use? Eight-ounce cups will mean that you can serve more cups of lemonade per pitcher. (If it's a gallon jug, with 64 ounces, then you can serve eight cups per pitcher. Sixteen-ounce cups, which may be perceived as a better value, means that you can serve only four per pitcher.)

     You must also decide what kind of lemonade to serve. Lemonade made from powdered concentrate is probably the cheapest – perhaps $1 a gallon. Lemonade made from fresh squeezed lemons has a definite quality advantage, but it's more expensive. At $0.25 a lemon and eight lemons to a gallon, it would cost $2 for each gallon. And you might be able to get prepackaged lemonade sold at the store for $1.50 a gallon.

Interviewer: So how long will it take me to get enough money for the earrings?

You: Assume $10 in sunk costs – $2 for the pitcher and $8 for 800 cups. You then need to decide what to charge. If you charge 50 cents a cup of lemonade – which I believe is the upward end of lemonade stand prices – and it costs you $1 to make the cheapest gallon of lemonade, then you'd earn $3 on each gallon of lemonade sold. In four weekends in three months, you would need to sell 37 gallons of lemonade. Then you'd earn $111 dollars – enough to pay off the pitcher and cups. That's three gallons a weekend, or 24 cups of lemonade each weekend.

Interviewer: Does this sound reasonable to you?

You: So far, yes. But this is just the cost-structure. You must consider other factors as well. Who are your competitors? Are there other kids trying to sell lemonade at the same time? Are you located near delis and restaurants and street vendors who might sell competing beverages?

What is the demand for your product? Is it summertime, when people drink a lot of lemonade and are spending time outdoors, generating foot traffic? If not, you may have difficulty moving your lemonade. In cold weather, you might want to consider selling hot cider instead.

Where are you located? How many potential customers will pass your lemonade stand? Can you set up your lemonade stand at a sporting event, supermarket parking lot, or flea market, where many more people will pass your stand? If you just set up on the sidewalk, you may not attract the foot traffic to make those numbers. Indoor or sheltered locations are also preferable if the weather turns bad.

You have a competitive advantage – you're young and cute. You may get business from people who approve of your young entrepreneurial actions. At the same time, lemonade stands have a reputation for relatively poor lemonade, which may hurt your overall sales if you have competition.

Hungry for more inside scoop? Join Vault.com's popular
online community for consulting — www.vault.com

VAULT.com   **83**

Do you have any subsidies? That is, would your dad be willing to cover your start-up costs – the pitcher, the cups, and perhaps the cost of the lemonade. This would perhaps permit you to offer better-quality lemonade.

Consider your advertising. You'll need a big sign to call attention to your stand. You can rely on your parents for free – I assume – word of mouth.

You should also consider offering another product besides lemonade. Perhaps selling cookies or brownies, in addition to the lemonade, might increase your profits.

You should consider other revenue-generating activities as well. If you are 14, a paper route is a possibility. You may also be old enough to babysit.

It's also possible that you might be able to choose another pair of earrings, or find the ones you want on sale. This would lower your income requirements.

6	Phoning in a Case

You are advising a credit card company that wants to market a prepaid phone card to its customers. Is this a good idea?

Whoa! Better find out more about this prepaid phone card first before you even begin to think about recommending the phone card.

You: What is the role of our company? Do we simply market the card or must we create them ourselves? Are we expected to provide the telephone services?

Interviewer: This card will be co-marketed with an outside phone company. We do not need to perform telecommunications functions.

You: What are our expenses connected with the card?

Interviewer: We must pay 15 cents for every minute we sell. We also have to pay $1.00 as a start-up cost for the card and card systems.

You: What are our marketing expenses?

Interviewer: We normally use slips of paper that are attached to the backs of our credit card payment envelopes. We sometimes also send customers a direct mailing – in a separate envelope. Or we can have telemarketers call selected customers.

You: What's the cost of each of these marketing techniques, and what is their response rate?

Interviewer: Telemarketers have a 2 percent response rate and cost $1.00 per call. Direct mailings cost us 40 cents per mailing and have a 0.50 percent rate of response. Our payment attachments have a 0.25 percent rate of response, but only cost us 5 cents each.

You: I'm going to assume we will sell one-hour phone cards. That will cost us $9.00 for the minutes and a dollar per card – so each card costs us $10.

Interviewer: Okay, that sounds reasonable.

You: And what is our expected revenue on a one-hour phone card? What is the current market rate for a 60-minute phone card?

Interviewer: Assume it's 50 cents a minute.

Hungry for more inside scoop? Join Vault.com's popular
online community for consulting — www.vault.com

VAULT.com   **85**

You: So if we sell the cards for $30, we have a $20 profit, minus our expenditures on marketing.

Interviewer: What's our cost structure look like?

You: Okay, let's figure this out.   To sell 1,000 cards through telemarketing, we would need to contact 50,000 people.   That would cost us $50,000.   To use direct mail, we would have to contact 200,000 thousand people, which, at 40 cents per mailing, costs us $80,000.   Since the envelope inserts aren't very reliable, we will need to contact 800,000 people using that method.   But at 5 cents each, it costs only $20,000 to sell 1,000 cards.

We make $20 profit on each card.   But even using the cheapest promotional vehicle, at $20 profit, we would only break even, because our profits on 1,000 cards would be $20,000.   We shouldn't market this card, unless we can further cut our marketing costs or increase the price of the card.   If we could slice the cost of the envelope attachments a penny or so, or sell the card for $35, or convince our co-marketer to reduce our costs, it might be worth selling.

Interviewer: What are some other issues you might want to consider? (Notice how the interviewer is nudging you to add to your analysis.)

You: We should also consider the competitive landscape for this business. Is the per-minute rate for calling card minutes expected to fall?   If so, and our costs are held constant, we may lose money.   Of course, we can learn more from marketing these cards.   It could be that the people likely to buy these cards might be frequent travelers and could be targeted for other promotions.

THINKING STRATEGICALLY

7	Inside Intel's Strategy

Why is Intel successful? Will they retain their advantage in the future?

Do you have a high-tech background? Does your interviewer want to see if you can think in broad strategic terms and if you've been following your industry? Then you might get a strategy analysis question like this one.

The interviewer is not expecting you to quote the latest stock price of Intel or know how much CEO Craig Barrett got paid last year. She wants you to explore what the company does right and the challenges that it faces in the future. Any business knowledge that you have will come in handy.

Well, what do you know about Intel? You should know that Intel is a producer of microprocessors (or chips), an essential component of computers. (That's about the level of knowledge you need.) Intel currently has about 80 percent of the microprocessor market. Clearly, they're doing something right, but what?

Intel is a technology company. In a rapidly evolving market like the computer industry, staying abreast of changes in technology is vital. You might point out that Intel's heavy investment in R&D has consistently enabled the company to produce better microprocessors than its competitors – and its headstart allows it to retain that R&D edge.

Intel's commanding lead in the market also allows the company to leverage its might to partner with its customers, ensuring they buy only Intel products. With 80 percent of the market, Intel has quite a bit of weight to throw around. And as such a high-volume producer, Intel has economies of scale: cost advantages and operating efficiencies its competitors can only dream of.

Intel has also successfully branded its products, the Pentium chips, so that customers know them by name and associate them with high quality. (It is unusual for a high-tech firm to brand itself so successfully. And remember all those "Intel Inside" logos? Intel partners with its customers in order to cross-promote its products.

Now you might point out Intel's weaknesses. Intel's competitors, like AMD and Cyrix, have managed to copy most of Intel's products (or surpass them in some instances). Intel has often succeeded by being first to market with its products. You might point out, however, that as society becomes more "wired," the major

Hungry for more inside scoop? Join Vault.com's popular
online community for consulting — www.vault.com

VAULT.com **87**

source of growth in the microchip market has been in lower-end, less-powerful chips – a market in which Intel's competitors are well-equipped to compete in price-sensitive markets. Already, many cheap computers rely on AMD and Cyrix chips. And the outcome of the antitrust suits both against Intel and Microsoft (Microsoft software runs on Intel chips) is a wild card.

8   Beam Me Up!

The Star Trek transporter has just been invented. Spell out some of the effects on the transportation industry.

Here's another (actual) case which calls for strategy analysis. First of all, remember not to make any assumptions. Don't apologize for not watching the show – ask your interviewer (who, if they've given you this question, is probably a fan) how exactly the transporter works. Effectively, the transporter is a near-instantaneous teleportation device. However, you should make sure you don't assume exactly what the transporter, as invented, can or can't do. (In this case, non-Trekkies may have an advantage!)

Let's see how this Q&A might proceed:

You: Um, could you tell me exactly how the transporter works? How much can it transport at one time?

Interviewer: Let's say the transporter can transport about the mass of Captain Kirk.

You: That would be about 200 pounds. Can it transport only living things, or inanimate objects as well?

Interviewer: Any type of object.

You: Can it transport anywhere at any time?

Interviewer: Yes.

You: Does there need to be another transporter at the end to receive the transport?

Interviewer: No, it's pretty much a one-way process.

You: How common are these devices? Are they going to be readily available to the average consumer? How much do they cost?

Interviewer: For the time being, the transporters are expensive. They would cost about $100,000 each.

You: That clearly takes them out of the range of most home users. How much does it cost to use them?

Interviewer: Assume that the marginal cost of a transport is near zero. The only cost is for the transport-operator time, which is relatively small.

You: Are they safe? You said they were just invented.

Interviewer: Except for the occasional freak accident, yes, they are safe. They are as safe as plane travel.

You: That makes them very safe indeed. Okay, what I'm going to do is analyze how transporters will affect the following transportation industries: cars, passenger airlines, cargo shipping and package transport.

Interviewer: Fine. Go ahead.

You: These transporters don't seem like they'll take the place of cars. They are too expensive for home use. Larger companies could afford them, however. I could see some companies buying transporters in order to transport their employees and clients back from the office. They would need a transporter chief, of course. So there might be some impact on commuter traffic – perhaps 10 to 20 percent. If mass transit systems adopt transporters as well, the impact on traffic may be greater.

On the other hand, the transporter is a terrific substitute for plane travel. It's instantaneous and from what you say, as safe as plane travel. The transporter will definitely be a serious competitor to airlines. Conceivably, passengers could be beamed directly to their destination, instead of going to the airport. The only drawback that I can see to the transporter is that any luggage would need to be beamed separately. And anyone weighing over 200 pounds may not be able to be beamed at all. This means that airplanes wouldn't disappear, but they would be used mostly for cargo transport and other heavier loads. They would probably serve fewer markets, as there would be much-reduced passenger travel to supplement their flights.

As far as cargo, I think ships and planes would still be used for most cargo transport. Two hundred pounds is too small an

Hungry for more inside scoop? Join Vault.com's popular
online community for consulting — www.vault.com

VAULT.com   **89**

amount for mass transport, and I'm assuming that you can't separate the contents of a transporter, that you can only beam stuff to one area at once.

Interviewer: That's how I understand it, yes.

You: Then getting packages sent same day, to anywhere in the world, would be a premium service. You could only ship one package at a time. You might be able to charge double or triple the price of an overnight package. Shipping companies like Federal Express might profit from its introduction.

9 | Market Entry

> **A multi-billion dollar consumer brand product manufacturer is considering introducing its flagship brand into Asia. What would you advise?**

This is an example of a broad question where you must first assess the situation in more detail. A series of "helicoptering" questions:

- Why has the company engaged our services?

- What are the risk factors associated with this project?

- What is the timing for our involvement with this client and this project?

- What is the nature of the client's business? What is their flagship brand?

- What business unit within the organization has engaged us?

You should have more information about the nature of the project after these questions. From here, you can pursue a more specific series of questions. Let's say that in response to your questions, you learn that the project involves a software package selection for automating trade promotions activity in preparation for entry into Asia. (Now you see why it's so important to ask questions) The next set of questions you should ask would be drilldowns – teasing out the finer points – on the information you've just gathered. For example:

- Have any vendors been identified for the selection? If so, whom?

- What is the timeframe for the package selection?

- What client staff will be participating in the project? What are their roles in the organization?

- What experience does the firm have with similar engagements/industries? Can we draw upon that experience for this engagement? Why or why not?

- Has a workplan been developed for this project? What is an overview of this plan?

- What are the measures that have been established to evaluate the success of this selection?

Hungry for more inside scoop? Join Vault.com's popular
online community for consulting — www.vault.com

V/\ULT.com **91**

USING THE FOUR Ps

10 Taking Wing

> It's 1982. You're a consultant sitting on the plane next to your client,
> who is the CEO of American Airlines. The client tells you that
> American can't seem to keep many repeat customers and wants to
> institute something called a "frequent flyer" program to reward loyal
> passengers with "points" they can redeem for free flights. He turns to
> you and asks you to analyze the merits and faults of the program. How
> do you respond?

This a good candidate for the Four P s framework. (Note that the interviewer has
deliberately set this case at a time when you cannot use online membership as a
substitute or addition.) A good analysis would tee off with some scoping
questions to understand the evolution of the idea:

• Are you aware of any programs currently in existence that caused you to
consider this idea for American Airlines? If so, what do you feel are major
advantages/disadvantages?

• Have you done any market research within your customer base to determine
how well this program would be received if instituted?

• Can you sketch the purchasing habits of your top flyers for me? How much do
they currently spend on air travel per year, what percentage is business vs.
leisure, are there a particular set of routes this group frequents, do they stick
with one airline or purchase tickets on many airlines, etc.?

• Would the current customer service business unit be charged with
implementing this program or would you consider investment in a separate
initiative?

Price
• Would there be a membership fee for this program? Would this program be
available to all American customers or only those who fly at or over a certain
threshold?

• Based on your customers' current flight habits, would you set milestones for
award redemption?

Product

- Would the program be based on miles, segments, price of tickets, or another factor?

- What need would this program satisfy that does not currently exist in the marketplace?

- Would there be any redemption restrictions based on route or day?

- What other rewards would be available to members besides flights? Special member lounges in airports? Car rentals? Hotel rooms?

- What would be accumulated – points, miles, levels?

- Would these accumulated criteria ever expire?

- Would you award extremely high-volume flyers with additional perks? What would they be? Would flyers have to re-earn this status or once attained would it be good for life?

Position/Place

- Are you aware of any similar programs in today's marketplace? If so, what would differentiate your program from others that already exist?

- Based on your knowledge of your customers' behavior, would you think that a frequent flyer program would induce high switching costs, such that it would make it difficult for high-volume customers to switch airlines due to the loss of miles/status with American?

Promotion

- How would you introduce this program to your customers? Through airports, the media, travel agents? Would it be available only to frequent flyers or all the flying public?

- How would customers sign up for this program? Would it be automatic, a form, a phone call to customer service?

- Would there ever be any promotional drives such as doubling awards or offering bundle pricing (such as two-for-one)?

Be careful of using historic precedent in historic cases. While frequent flyer miles are a fact of business history, your analysis might show that the long-term benefits are not worth the creation of the program.

Hungry for more inside scoop? Join Vault.com's popular
online community for consulting — www.vault.com

VAULT.com   **93**

SAILING THE FIVE Cs

11 **You have the opportunity to purchase a landscaping business. How would you decide whether or not to buy it, and how much to pay for it?**

This question is a good candidate for the Five Cs. Determine:

Character

- How would you evaluate the sincerity, honesty, and integrity of the owner of the business? Do others that they deal with (employees, suppliers, customers) value them as partners, or are there character issues?

- Is there any legal action pending against the business?

- Does the business have a positive employee culture? Does it engage in any charitable or environmental initiatives?

Capacity

- Is the business turning away new customers due to lack of equipment/ employees?

- Are the assets of the company (property, plant) strained or in a state of disrepair?

Capital

- Is the landscaping business carrying any debt? What is its debt ratio?

- What is the company's cash flow like over the last five years?

- What is the company's new account history? How much business is new vs. repeat?

Collateral

- Are any of the business' assets impaired in any way? Obsolete equipment, for instance?

Conditions

- Describe the market space the business occupies. Is it a leader? Are there many players?

- What defines dominance in this market? Cost? Economies of scale? Speed to market? Relationships with customers? Where does this business fall against the aforementioned metrics?

- Is the market for landscaping saturated? Are there opportunities for expanding the current customer base?

- What advertising and promotional activity has been done? How much does the business spend (as a percent of sales) on marketing its services?

---

12 **You have inherited a start-up software company. How do you estimate market size? On which fronts do you anticipate problems?**

Another great candidate for the Five Cs. Here are some points adjusted for the unique dynamics of the start-up environment.

Character

- How would you evaluate the sincerity, honesty, and integrity of the owner of the business? Do others that they deal with (employees, suppliers, customers) value them as partners or are there character issues?

- Is there any legal action pending against the business?

- Does the mission of the start-up make sense? Is it business concept sound?

- What is the timeline/progress of development, coding, testing, and production as originally conceived in the business plan? Does it make sense?

- What is the previous track record of each of the principals of the startup?

Capacity

- What is the plan for producing the product when the code is ready? Is outsourcing stamping, packaging, and shipping an option?

Capital

- What is the makeup of the initial seed capital to start the business? Personal assets, small business loan, venture capital funds?

- What is the debt structure like if it exists? Interest rates, due dates, rollover ability, secured assets, etc.?

Hungry for more inside scoop? Join Vault.com's popular
online community for consulting — www.vault.com

VAULT.com **95**

Collateral

- Have any patents been applied for? What is their status?

- What has been done to protect the intellectual capital/property associated with the software design?

Conditions

- Describe the market space the business occupies. Why did the business come into inception?

- What defines dominance in this market? Cost? Economies of scale? Speed to market? Relationships with customers? Where does this business fall against the aforementioned metrics?

- Is the market for this type of product saturated? Is there a particular unfulfilled segment where this product fits, or will it be competing against other already established products?

- What is the advertising and promotional activity planned for this product?

13 Distribution Case

We have been engaged by a major entertainment company to assist them in building a distribution network for home video. They currently contract their distribution through other, more established, entities but the contracts with those companies are expiring and it is unclear whether the new contracts contain favorable terms or not. There is still a chance that our client may continue to distribute their products through a third party. How would you assess whether to build a distribution network or continue the contracts with the third parties?

First of all, you need to ask your interviewer some basic questions:

- It makes sense to ask your interviewer about best practices – that is, what are other entertainment companies doing? What are the current costs? Does the company have the staff and resources to create its own distribution network?

- Of the major entertainment companies that produce video, do most distribute through their own proprietary supply chain or through third parties?

- What is the client's current cost of distribution through its contractual partner(s)?

- Has the client attempted to assess building its own distribution network before retaining us? If so, what were its findings?

- Does the client have a dedicated functional staff assigned to the project? If so, what functional areas do they represent?

After establishing some basic facts, it's time to get more detailed. Your interviewer may allude to certain avenues to discuss, or shut down others. If the interviewer confirms that, yes, the company does have enough current staff to handle setting up its own network, there's no call to delve deeper into the ramifications of reassigning personnel. Let's say that, through questioning, you've come to decide that staying with a third-party distributor makes the most sense. Now the question is – should the company stay with its current distributor, or choose a new one?

- Who are possible alternative partners? Who uses them?

- Could you characterize the relationship between the client's distribution partner and the client? Is there a possibility of retaliation on the part of the distribution partner if the client severs its ties to this party?

- How many weeks of supply are currently in the distribution partner's pipeline?

- How receptive are the client's accounts to changing distribution partners? Has a value proposition been created to show the client's accounts that a client-owned supply chain would be more efficient, valuable, etc. to the accounts?

- Does the client have any financial interest in the distribution partner that might have to be severed?

After answering these questions, make a recommendation.

Hungry for more inside scoop? Join Vault.com's popular
online community for consulting — www.vault.com

VAULT.COM   **97**

14 A Powerful Case

You're a utilities company in a small town and you're having trouble getting your customers to pay on time. What do you do?

First of all, you'll need to know what kind of company you are. Electric? Gas? Phone? Could it be that you are based in a small, rural area where customers turn to their wood-burning stoves for heat and cooking power instead of gas? Have your customers adopted cell phones en masse and are now neglecting their regular phone bills? You won't know until you pin down the problem – and then you can determine a solution for the company's woes.

Some questions you should ask:

- Where are we based?
- What is the composition of our customer base?
- What percentage of our customers are not paying on time?
- How much money do we lose from slow payers?
- How many of those slow payers never pay?
- Is there a certain segment of the population that is not paying?
- Is the area in a recession or slump that affects the ability of customers to pay their bills?
- How late are the payments of the slow payers?
- What do we currently do to motivate slow payers to pay their bills?
- Are there any government or state regulations that will affect our actions?
- At what point do we currently cut off slow payers? (Perhaps the company is so slow to do so that customers are taking advantage of the company. Or, if the town is small enough, it's possible that there are employees who refuse to cut off power to their friends and family.)

After you've determined the nature of the problem, you can make a recommendation on how to solve it. You may have more than one problem. Perhaps your small town is home to a university, and students move frequently and often neglect their last utilities bills. (Can you work out an arrangement with the university that denies diplomas or registration to students that neglect their bills? Should you start asking for second and third addresses and contact numbers? Perhaps requiring a deposit from students to turn on power?) At the same time, your company may need to start charging higher late fees to other customers who are simply taking advantage of the six months of forgiveness your utility gives.

15 | Under Pressure

While most interviewers will be pleasant, there are some interviews that are seemingly designed to be stressful. Here's an actual example of how one "pressure case" started off:

Interviewer: Okay, what kind of case do you want?

Candidate: Huh?

Interviewer: We don't have much time. Give me a case.

Candidate: Um, market entry?

Interviewer: Okay. Truck leasing.

Candidate: What?

Interviewer: Truck leasing. Europe.

Candidate: Well, what countries in Europe are we targeting?

Interviewer: Wrong!

Candidate: (Taken aback) Who are our competitors?

Interviewer: Wrong.

Candidate: What kinds of trucks do we lease?

Interviewer: Wrong, wrong.

Candidate: I give up!

Interviewer: What is truck leasing?

It goes to show – you can never make assumptions in case interviews! Even if you think you know what truck leasing, or shrimp farming, or any other industry you're presented with – don't proceed without clarifying your suppositions with the interviewer.

Hungry for more inside scoop? Join Vault.com's popular
online community for consulting — www.vault.com

VΛULT.com   **99**

A WRITTEN CASE

Some cases are written and do not involve an interactive process between the interviewer and the candidate. (Monitor uses written cases frequently, for example.) Here's an example of an actual written case, and a potential outline.

16 "Widget Associates is a private equity placement firm with $3 billion in assets. They are primarily focused on the confluence of information and high technology and would like to utilize their assets in a manner consistent with this interest. Below, please describe your approach to the following:

   • **Assessing Widget Associates' strategic direction**

   • **Evaluating its market interest and its potential for success**

   • **Creating a value proposition that marries its strategic vision with marketplace dynamics**

   • **Suggestions for initial placement of funds**

Please be succinct with your answers. You may bullet point if you like. You have 30 minutes to complete the exercise."

The best way to approach written business case questions is to create a brief outline and then flesh out those points. Don't write too much, or in too much detail. This is a very easy mistake to make since you will be nervous and under time pressure. The art of answering written case interview questions successfully is to be succinct, logical, and speedy. An appropriate outline to use as a framework for this answer might be:

1) Strategic assessment

   (a) Industry assessment

   (b) Key members, market potential/forecast, volatility

   (c) Tools to use (Porter's Five Forces, BCG Matrix, etc.)

   (d) Widget's potential for a role in this industry

   (e) Risk assessment

2) Value Proposition

(a) Assessment of the value Widget brings to this industry

(b) Justification for injection of outside funds into this industry

3) Tactical effort

(a) Identification of a short list of primary targets

(b) Assess readiness of key players (management team, legal, financial, etc.)

(c) Evaluate all potential marketplace outcomes and validate against strategy

(d) Construction of workplan with milestones/deadlines and go/no decision points

This is probably an overly detailed outline but you may choose to answer the question simply as above, with a little bit of detail attached to each sub-point. Remember that the interviewer isn't looking for The Great American Novel, or even flashes of what you perceive as wit. Just the actions you would take to assess, evaluate, analyze, and recommend action for the situation.

THE FINANCIAL CASE INTERVIEW

Case interviews aren't just for consultants any more. Many investment banks give questions that could, under other circumstances, be called case interviews – they often involve both strategy and quantitative know-how. Consulting firms often use similar cases. Here are a few such questions.

17   **What is a company that you follow closely? Is it a good investment?**

Tell your interviewer you would look at various criteria to determine if it's a worthwhile investment, including:

- **Earnings growth:**   Determine how fast the company's earnings are expected to grow, looking at the following factors (among others): the company's historic growth rate; earnings growth rates of other companies in the industry; growth rate of the market the company services; analyst estimates; and perhaps building your own financial model in Excel to test various assumptions.

Hungry for more inside scoop? Join Vault.com's popular
online community for consulting — www.vault.com

VAULT.com   **101**

- **Industry analysis:** Evaluate the industry the company is in to determine whether this is an attractive industry in which to invest. Look at factors including: how rapidly the industry is growing; whether the industry is consolidating; how intense the competition is among competitors; whether market players have pricing power; and whether products are considered commodities.

- **Competitive advantages:** Evaluate whether the company has any competitive advantages over its competition, such as patents, exclusive contracts, a differentiated product, brand equity, a lower cost structure, or superior management.

- **Valuation:** Given its prospects, is the company a good value? You would compare the company's expected earnings growth to various valuation measures, like price-to-earnings ratio, price-to-sales ratio, and price-to-book-value. You would also compare these valuation measures to other companies in the industry to determine whether the company is relatively expensive or relatively affordable.

- **Portfolio considerations:** Finally, you would want to determine whether an investment in the company fits well with your overall portfolio and objectives. You would want to ask questions like: Does the company help diversify risk in your portfolio? Does the company meet your portfolio's risk profile?

THE M&A CASE

18 You represent a major food manufacturer. You have been asked to assess the potential acquisition of a premium priced flour company based in the Southeast. The asking price is $130 million. The company's profit after tax this year is $11.2 million. You have audited financial information and you can do interviews.

First, assess whether the asking price of $130 million is in the ballpark of reason, and determine what the target's value is to your client.

Calculate the baseline value – the value of the company with constant margins and zero growth. The value of the company (or net present value) = cash flow/ discount rate. (Cash Flow = Net Income – Capital Expenditures + Depreciation +/- Changes in Working Capital)

At zero growth, Cap X should equal depreciation, and the working capital will be stable. Therefore, Cash Flow = Net Operating Profit after Tax.

Cash Flow divided by the discount rate is the net present value (Let's say the discount rate is 0.10. if your interviewer asks, tell him you would calculate the discount rate using the Capital Asset Pricing Model). Let's say Cash Flow divided by the discount rate is $112 million. Assuming $8 million in goodwill tax write-offs, the total baseline value is $120.

What is the market position of the flour company? Let's say your interviewer gives you this chart:

Flour Share
Target's 3-State Market Area

Now you must ask your interviewer questions to supplement your knowledge about the flour company.

You: Will price increases be sustainable? How much will prices increase per year? How modern are the facilities?

Interviewer: Price increases have been seen every year and prices will probably continue to rise over the next five years, 2 to 3 percent per year.

You: Will further expansion into other markets be possible? What is the firm's share in non-core markets?

Interviewer: Less than 2 percent. While the firm has expanded into non-core markets, advertising and marketing costs are very high. Share gains are possible but slowly and at a lower margin than existing businesses.

What are the possible synergies with the food manufacturer? Sketch out a chart:

Potential Synergy	NPV Impact ($M)	Probability	NPV Impact x Probability ($M)
Economies of scale in purchasing	20.0	60%	12.0
Leverage distribution capabilities in outlying markets	12.0	70%	8.4
Leverage know-how to improve revenue realization for by-product	14.0	70%	9.8
Provide learning experience in value-added consumer products	?	?	?
		Total	**30.2**

The baseline value is $120 million. While it is uncertain how much upside there will be in market expansion, synergies are likely to be at least $30 million.

From this you can ascertain:

The flour business is mature, but secure. Its volume declines are set off by price increases. Its brand position should allow a price premium. The flour business is a good buy.

PRACTICE M&A CASES

19 Eastern Newspapers is a large newspaper chain that is considering diversifying into non-newspaper media assets and is a potential client for our firm's M&A group. How would you go about advising this client? What information would you want to gather before you meet with the client?

Notes:

20 JerseyWeb is a small Internet access provider, with $20 million in annual revenues. JerseyWeb is considering acquiring another small Internet access provider in nearby Connecticut. What would you advise JerseyWeb to do?

Notes:

Hungry for more inside scoop? Join Vault.com's popular
online community for consulting — www.vault.com

VAULT.com **105**

21 A major ski resort currently forbids snowboarding, but is considering allowing the sport. What should it consider before allowing or disallowing snowboarding?

Notes:

22 The maple syrup market has four main competitors. The market share and price per unit are as follows.

Absolute Syrup	share 42 percent	price per unit	$5.00
Beastly Syrup	share 27 percent	price per unit	$4.10
Catchall Syrup	share 16 percent	price per unit	$3.50
Delight Syrup	share 15 percent	price per unit	$3.55

What kind of market is this?

Notes:

23 You are Britney Spears. You are afraid that the new craze for MP3s will hurt sales of your music. What should you do?

Notes:

Hungry for more inside scoop? Join Vault.com's popular
online community for consulting — www.vault.com

VAULT.COM **107**

ADDITIONAL PRACTICE QUESTIONS

24 Ch-Ch-Chain (of Rental Cars)

You have been appointed the manager of a rental car company. How do you measure its efficiency?

This case question is a good candidate for the Value Chain approach.

- What are your expenses (cars, insurance, rental of car office, advertising)?

- What is your average rental time period? (On average how long is a car checked out?)

- How fast is a vehicle turned around (from drop-off to back on the line)? What is the industry average for this turnaround?

- What percentage of your fleet is down for repairs on average? How does this compare to the industry?

- What percentage of your employees call out sick every day on average? How does this compare to the industry?

- Does the business exhibit any seasonality (for example, are you located near a ski resort that sees business boom in the winter)? How do you account for these effects?

Another way to look at this question is to use a real-life "out-of-the-box" approach. Why not simply look out on the lot and see how many cars are rented out at any given time, and what kind they are – and do this over a period of time in different locations? This kind of real-world approach will win points with consultants, who actually have to drive around and look at parking lots at 4 a.m. (and other such hijinx) more often than they would probably like.

25 Our client has engaged us to assist them in reorganizing their sales force. They want to cut $50 million in costs from this area over the next two years.

This is an organizational change question. What is especially important here is to balance the financial realities of the situation against the organization impact of head count reduction, the introduction of new technologies, etc. Questions that would help focus this situation include:

- What is the primary business for this client?

- What is the timeline for the reorganization process?

- What is the early estimate of how many people could be involved?

- What is the scope of change? Does it include downsizing, the introduction of technologies, closing/selling-off of locations, reengineering business processes?

- What is the early assessment of the organizational climate for change? Are they receptive or resistive? What are the reasons for resistance if any?

- Can you describe any dynamics unique to this client's business that put the success of the project at risk?

- What are the major risk factors surrounding this project?

- What are the measurements of success for this project?

26 Your client is trying to decide whether or not to invest in a helicopter company. You have been asked to assess the long-term attractiveness of the helicopter market.

Since this case is primarily asking for an industry analysis (is this an attractive industry?), Porter's Five Forces is one framework useful in formulating your recommendation.

Hungry for more inside scoop? Join Vault.com's popular
online community for consulting — www.vault.com

VAULT.com **109**

27 **A large health care company has hired you to determine a strategy for improving profitability through growth. The company hopes to reach its goal in three years. What do you advise?**

Note that your interviewer will often impose deadlines and other "constraints" that represent the wishes of the client (for example, the client wants to reach its goal within six months; the company wants to reach its goal without spending more than $5 million; etc.). You should not necessarily be constrained by the company's hoped-for timelines or budget constraints, unless your interviewer tells you otherwise. In this case, you should question whether three years is a realistic or even optimal timeline. Your job is to recommend the best course of action, including an optimal timeline, not to take your client's wishes as representing the best course of action.

28 **Our client, ABC Airlines, is losing money. Why?**

Remember to consider the firm's actions as well as external market forces such as the competitive environment. Questions include asking whether other airlines are losing money, or suffering drops in profits. If so, why? Causes might range from a rise in the cost of fuel, to the need to replace most of ABC's fleet due to stringent new government regulations, to a general slump in the economy that reduces the number of tourists and causes business customers to tighten their belts.

29 **You are head of a large American corporation. Your company must build a new paper plant. You must decide which country to build the plant in. What factors would you consider?**

Analyze your supply chain. Where do you incur your costs? If your paper plant is highly automated, it might make more sense to build it in America or another developed country where you have access to skilled labor. If, on the other hand, your paper plant requires thousand of employees, you may want to consider a country or region of America where the cost of labor is lower.

30   Your client is a major airline that wants to reduce the amount of money it spends per passenger on food service, ticketing, and baggage handling. What would you advise?

Benchmarking is one good starting point for this type of case. You would certainly want to know (or at least be able to estimate) how much other airlines spend on each passenger for food service, ticketing, and baggage handling. Are your client's costs in each of these areas high or low for the industry?

You would also want to examine "best practices": which airlines have the lowest costs in each of the three areas of food service, ticketing, and baggage handling? What are they doing right, and how can we emulate it? (Remember that best practices for a particular process may be found outside the airline industry. For example, how do passenger railroads or cruise ships ticket their passengers? Are companies in that industry doing anything particularly well that may apply to the airline business?)

GUESSTIMATES

"Guesstimate" case interviews

Guesstimate questions are among the most unnerving questions you may ever have to answer in an interview situation. They can be so "off the wall" as to shake up an otherwise calm, collected candidate.

The approach to guesstimates is basically the same as business cases – you will showcase your ability to analyze a situation and form conclusions about this situation by thinking out loud. The difference here is that you will not necessarily be using a series of questions to gather feedback from the interviewer. Instead, you will drive toward a conclusion through a series of increasingly specific statements. Let's look at an example:

How many ping-pong balls fit in a 747?

No, this isn't a joke. This is an actual question used in consulting interviews. If you are a little unsettled by this type of question, it's no wonder. That is exactly the reaction the interviewer is expecting. Remember that the main objective of these questions is to evaluate your poise and professionalism when facing an outlandish situation. How you react to this question when presented will speak volumes about your ability to be professional when faced with a similar business situation at a client.

So, how do you approach a guesstimate question? First, do NOT panic. If you are visibly shaken when presented with a guesstimate or brainteaser, it will hurt you. It is extremely important that you do not lose your cool.

Do not let yourself struggle verbally. You are free to say something like, "That is an intriguing question. May I have a moment to think it through?" This statement immediately shows the interviewer you are still in control and gives you some breathing time to think about a method for answering.

Once you have had a minute to compose your thoughts, be sure and go through your reasoning out loud, so your interviewer can see that you're arriving at your answer in a logical manner. "Don't be anal," suggests one former consultant. "You should realize that for the purposes of a guesstimate, 1,000,553 is the same as a million, and you can divide by 350 if you need to divide by the number of days in the year."

Finally, remember that there is no right answer for guesstimates. It will often not even be necessary to come up with a definitive response like "1,400,350," due to constraints on time. Always work toward a final answer, but do not feel that you have done a poor job if the interviewer moves on to other topics before you are finished. They may simply recognize that you're on the right track and see no reason to keep going.

Acing guesstimates

The best approach for a guesstimate or brainteaser question is to think of a funnel. You begin by thinking broadly, then slowly drill down towards the answer. Let's look at this approach in context. Referring to our sample question, you know that you are looking for how many ping-pong balls fit in a 747 airplane. The first thing you need to determine is the volume of the ping-pong ball.

For any guesstimate or brainteaser question you will need to understand whether your interviewer will be providing any direction or whether you will have to make assumptions. Therefore, begin the analysis of a guesstimate or brainteaser question with a question to your interviewer, such as, "What is the volume of a single ping pong ball?" If the interviewer does not know or refuses to provide any answer, then you will know that you must assume the answer. If the interviewer does provide the information, then your approach will be a series of questions. For this example let's assume your interviewer wants you to make the assumptions. Your verbal dialogue might go something like this:

Let's assume that the volume of a ping-pong ball is three cubic inches. Now let's assume that all the seats in the plane are removed. We'll say the average person is six feet high, one foot wide and one foot deep. That's 6 cubic feet, or 10,368 cubic inches. (One cubic foot is 12x12x12 inches, or 1,728 cubic inches.)

Okay, so a 747 has about 400 seats in it, excluding the galleys, lavatories, and aisles on the lower deck and about 25 seats on the upper deck. Let's assume there are three galleys, 14 lavatories, and three aisles (two on the lower deck and one on the upper deck), and that the space occupied by the galleys is a six-person equivalent, by the lavatories is a two-person equivalent, and the aisles are a 50-person equivalent on the lower deck and a 20-person equivalent on the upper deck. That's an additional 18, 28, and 120 person-volumes for the remaining space. We won't include the cockpit since someone has to fly the plane. So there are about 600 person-equivalents available. (You would be rounding a bit to make your life easier, since the actual number is 591 person equivalents.)

In addition to the human volume, we have to take into account all the cargo and extra space – the belly holds, the overhead luggage compartments, and the space over the passengers' head. Let's assume the plane holds four times the amount of extra space as it does people, so that would mean extra space

Hungry for more inside scoop? Join Vault.com's popular
online community for consulting — www.vault.com

VAULT.com **115**

is 2,400 person-equivalents in volume. (Obviously, this assumption is the most important factor in this guesstimate. Remember that it's not important that this assumption be correct, just that you know the assumption should be made.)

Therefore, in total we have 3,000 (or 600 + 2,400) person-equivalents in volume available. Three thousand x 10,368 cubic inches means we have 31,104,000 cubic inches of space available. At three cubic inches per ball, a 747 could hold 10,368,000 balls. However, spheres do not fit perfectly together. Eliminate a certain percentage – spheres cover only about 70 percent of a cube when packed – and cut your answer to 7,257,600 balls.

You might be wondering how you would calculate all these numbers in your head! No one expects you to be a human calculator, so you should be writing down these numbers as you develop them. Then you can do the math on paper, in front of the interviewer, which will further demonstrate your analytical abilities.

You choose the numbers, so pick nice round numbers that are easy for you to manipulate. Even if you just read a study that states that there are 270 million inhabitants in the United States, no interviewer will flinch if you estimate the number of American inhabitants as 300 million.

QUICK GUESSTIMATE NUMBERS

You'll need to grab numbers for guesstimates quickly. Here are some basic stats.

There are approximately 260 million people in the United States (but you can round up to 300 million for the purposes of guesstimates). By comparison, there are 1.2 billion people in China.

There are about 100 million households in the United States.

There are 60 million people online in the United States.

According to Gemini Consulting, 89 percent of all Web users have English as a first language.

Forrester Research estimates that by 2003, $3.2 trillion dollars will be spent on e-commerce online.

There are approximately nine million people in New York City, 13 million people in Shanghai, 3.5 million people in Los Angeles and eight million in London, England.

The extra step

Don't forget to add the "extra step" into your guesstimate. If you're trying to figure out how many blocks there are in New York City, remember to eliminate blocks covered by Central Park (and other parks). If you're determining the number of black cars in the United States, once you've estimated the number of cars in America, make sure you estimate what percentage of them are black.

In-case guesstimates

Not all guesstimates are stand-alone questions. Many are contained within case questions, mostly in the form of a market sizing. (And what would you say is the size of the market for pork rinds in the United States?) The key here is to derive a reasonable (and easily manipulated) figure for your calculations.

Hungry for more inside scoop? Join Vault.com's popular
online community for consulting — www.vault.com

VAULT.com **117**

PRACTICE GUESSTIMATE QUESTIONS

Following are examples of guesstimates and suggested solutions. There is more variation here than in business cases. Whereas in business cases we ask that you make no assumptions, here you may have to make assumptions if your interviewer does not provide any additional information.

Remember to ask your interviewer each time you begin a guesstimate answer if they will provide information or if you will need to make assumptions. If you do, be sure to be perfectly clear where and when you are making assumptions.

This set of questions can be presented as either assumptive or with feedback from the interviewer.

---

1   **How many gallons of white house paint are sold in the U.S. every year?**

THE "START BIG" APPROACH: If you're not sure where to begin, start with the basic assumption that there are 270 million people in the U.S. (or 25 million businesses, depending on the question). If there are 270 million people in the United States, perhaps half of them live in houses (or 135 million people). The average family size is about three people, so there would be 45 million houses in the United States. Let's add another 10 percent to that for second houses and houses used for other purposes besides residential. So there are about 50 million houses.

If houses are painted every 10 years, on average (notice how we deftly make that number easy to work with), then there are 5 million houses painted every year. Assuming that one gallon of paint covers 100 square feet of wall, and that the average house has 2,000 square feet of wall to cover, then each house needs 20 gallons of paint. So 100 million gallons of paint are sold per year (5 million houses x 20 gallons). (Note: If you want to be fancy, you can ask your interviewer whether you should include inner walls as well!) If 80 percent of all houses are white, then 80 million gallons of white house paint are sold each year. (Don't forget that last step!)

THE "START SMALL" APPROACH: You could also start small, and take a town of 27,000 (about 1/10,000 of the population). If you use the same assumption that half the town lives in houses in groups of three, then there are 4,500 houses, plus another 10 percent, then there are really 5,000 houses to worry about. Painted every 10 years, 500 houses are being painted in any given year. If each house has 2,000 square feet of wall, and each gallon of paint covers 100 square feet, then each house needs 20 gallons – and so 10,000 gallons of house paint are sold each year in your typical town. Perhaps 8,000 of those are white. Multiply by 10,000 – you have 80 million gallons.

Your interviewer may then ask you how you would actually get that number, on the job, if necessary. Use your creativity – contacting major paint producers would be smart, putting in a call to HUD's statistics arm could help, or even conducting a small sample of the second calculation in a few representative towns is possible.

2   What is the size of the market for disposable diapers in China?

Here's a good example of a market sizing. How many people live in China? A billion. Because the population of China is young, a full 600 million of those inhabitants might be of child-bearing age. Half are women, so there are about 300 million Chinese women of childbearing age. Now, the average family size in China is restricted, so it might be 1.5 children, on average, per family. Let's say two-thirds of Chinese women have children. That means that there are about 300 million children in China. How many of those kids are under the age of two? About a tenth, or 30 million. So there are at least 30 million possible consumers of disposable diapers.

To summarize:

$$1 \text{ billion people}$$
$$\text{x} \quad 60\% \text{ childbearing age}$$
$$= \quad 600,000,000 \text{ people}$$
$$\text{x} \quad 1/2 \text{ are women}$$

$$= \quad 300,000,000 \text{ women of childbearing age}$$
$$\text{x} \quad 2/3 \text{ have children}$$

$$= \quad 200,000,000 \text{ women with children}$$
$$\text{x} \quad 1.5 \text{ children each}$$

$$= \quad 300,000,000 \text{ children}$$
$$\text{x} \quad 1/10 \text{ under age 2}$$
$$= \quad 30 \text{ million children}$$

Hungry for more inside scoop? Join Vault.com's popular
online community for consulting — www.vault.com

VAULT.com   **119**

3 | **How many square feet of pizza are eaten in the United States each month?**

Take your figure of 300 million people in America. How many people eat pizza? Let's say 200 million. Now let's say the average pizza-eating person eats pizza twice a month, and eats two slices at a time. That's four slices a month. If the average slice of pizza is perhaps six inches at the base and 10 inches long, then the slice is 30 square inches of pizza. So four pizza slices would be 120 square inches. Therefore, there are a billion square feet of pizza eaten every month.

To summarize:

300 million people in America

200 million eat pizza

Average slice of pizza is six inches at the base and 10 inches long = 30 square inches (height x half the base)

Average American eats four slices of pizza a month

Four pieces x 30 square inches = 120 square inches (one square foot is 144 inches), so let's assume one square foot per person

200 million square feet a month

4 | **How many pay phones are there on the island of Manhattan?**

There are two ways to handle this problem. First of all, you could estimate how many blocks there are in Manhattan, and assume that 75 percent of all blocks have a pay phone. (Remember, the interviewer didn't say they had to work.) If there are about 15 avenues across Manhattan, and if the island is 300 streets long, then there are about 4,500 intersections. If every intersection indicates a block, then there are 4,500 blocks in the city. That means 3,000 pay phones. Now add the extra step and subtract the size of Central Park. Say that Central Park is 50 streets by six avenues – that means you lose 300 blocks, or 200 pay phones. You have the figure of 2,800 pay phones. Now estimate how many pay phones exist in bars, restaurants, schools, etc. There may be a total of 3,500 pay phones in Manhattan. (This question is also sometimes used with estimating the number of manhole covers in Manhattan.)

5   **How many weddings are performed each day in Japan?**

Try a ground-up approach. In a city of 1 million (Kyoto), how many people are of marriageable age? Let's say 750,000. How many get married in a given year? Maybe 2 percent? That's 15,000. Now, the population of Japan is about 200 million, so multiply 15,000 by 200 – and you get 300,000 weddings every year. Divide that by 365 and you get 822 weddings per day (on the average, though clearly some days are more popular than others). To estimate this in your head, you could divide 300,000 by 3,000 (getting 1,000), then take off another fifth. Around 800 would be close.

To summarize:

1 million people in Kyoto

750,000 of marriageable age

2 percent get married in the average year

750,000 x 0.02 = 15,000 marriages every year in Kyoto

200 million people in Japan

200 x 15,000 = 300,000 weddings per year

300,000/365 = 822 weddings per day (or approximately 800)

6   **How would you estimate the weight of the Chrysler building?**

This is a process guesstimate – the interviewer wants to know if you know what questions to ask. First, you would find out the dimensions of the building (height, weight, depth). This will allow you to determine the volume of the building. Does it taper at the top? (Yes.) Then, you need to estimate the composition of the Chrysler building. Is it mostly steel? Concrete? How much would those components weigh per square inch? Remember the extra step – find out whether you're considering the building totally empty or with office furniture, people, etc? (If you're including the contents, you might have to add 20 percent or so to the building's weight.)

Hungry for more inside scoop? Join Vault.com's popular
online community for consulting — www.vault.com

VΛULT.com **121**

7   **How many children are born every day in the United States?**

Population of United States: 300 million (approximately). Half are women (150 million). Perhaps half of those are of childbearing age. How do you determine how many women are pregnant at any given time? Well:

Let's say the average span of childbearing for a woman is 40 years

The average woman has two children

So a woman is pregnant one year in 20, or 5 percent of the time

3.75 million women are pregnant every year

So divide by 365 – you get about 10,000 babies a day (actually, 10,273)

Do the extra step – round up for multiple births, so maybe 12,000

8   **How much change would you find on the floor of an average mall?**

This seemingly silly guesstimate was received by a job seeker at McKinsey. It's an example of a guesstimate that is also a way to test candidate's "out-of-the-box" thinking. First, estimate how many stores there are in the average mall – say, 50. Now, how many people enter the average store on the average day? A thousand? So if there are 50,000 visitors to a mall daily, how many lose change? If one in 50, say, drops money (1,000 people a day), how much is the average loss of change? Most amounts are probably small. People carry fewer quarters, for example, and are more likely to retrieve them. So let's say that if a person is equally likely to drop a penny, nickel, or dime, then the average person who loses change loses a nickel. That means there would be $500 worth of change on the average floor. If half of that change has been picked up immediately, that would be $250 worth of change.

Also ask: Is there a fountain in the mall? If a fountain is considered to be the "floor" of the mall, the amount of change would obviously increase.

9   How many bottles of wine are consumed in the United States each week?

Determine:

1. The number of people in the United States

2. The number of adults

3. The number of wine drinkers

4. Average number of glasses of wine consumed per wee.

5. Number of glasses of wine in an average bottle

(Extra step: You may wish to estimate how much wine is used for non-drinking purposes – cooking, for example. Also clarify whether the interviewer is speaking of standard-sized bottle of wine.)

You could reasonably make the following assumptions:

There are about 300 million people in the United States:

250 million are adults

Perhaps 220 million drink alcohol

200 million drink wine

The average wine drinker drinks two glasses of wine a week,

400 million glasses of wine consumers per week

About five glasses of wine in the average bottle

80 million bottles of wine consumed in America each week

Estimate how many bottles wine is used for cooking – perhaps another 5 million

85 million bottles of wine consumed per week

Hungry for more inside scoop? Join Vault.com's popular
online community for consulting — www.vault.com

VAULT.com **123**

OTHER GUESSTIMATES...

> **10** **How many men's suits were sold in the United States last year?**

Determine:

1. Estimate the population of the United States.

2. Cut that in half to get the number of men.

3. Determine how many men are employed in occupations which require business attire.

4. Determine how many suits the average business attire employee would have purchased (due to weather, fashion changes, cleanings, wear, etc.).

5. Assume (or ask) a number of suits that those men not employed in business attire jobs purchased for religious, social, or other reasons.

6. Sum up the number and present your answer.

To summarize:

Population of the United States: 270 million (or 300 million, to round up).

Half are men – 150 million.

Let's say two-thirds are employed,

150 million x 2/3 = 100 million

Assume every employed man owns one suit = 100 million suits.

Estimate that about a quarter of men are in a field where they must own more than one suit.

If each of those men has an additional two suits, 25 million men x 2 additional suits = 50 million suits,

150 million suits in the United States.

How often does the average suit-owner replace a suit? Perhaps once every three years.

There are 50 million suits sold every year in the United States.

11   How many tennis balls fit in a swimming pool?

Determine:

1. What is the shape and depth of the swimming pool?

2. What is the volume of a tennis ball?

3. Estimate the volume of the swimming pool based on the depth, length, and width of the pool.

4. Calculate the number of balls by dividing the volume of the pool by the volume of the tennis ball.

5. You may wish to subtract balls due to steps in the pool and the gradual upslope of the pool due to the varying depth (but ask first).

12   How many windows are there on one of the Twin Towers?

Determine:

1. How many floors does the building have?

2. How many windows are on one face of the building?

3. Multiply the number of windows per face by four and then by the number of floors.

13   How many gas stations are there in Los Angeles?

Determine:

1. What is the population of Los Angeles?

2. What is the number of cars in Los Angeles? What is the average number of cars per person (including commuters)?

3. How many gas stations are needed per car?

14 **What is the annual size of the golf ball market in the United States? What factors drive demand?**

Determine:

1. What is the population of U.S.?

2. What percentage of the population golfs?

3. How often does the average golfer golf?

4. What is the number of balls used in an average golf game (and number that are lost)?

What factors drive demand?

• How many golf courses are being built in the United States?

• How many are planned?

• Is the population of golfers (due to Tiger Woods and his ilk) expanding?

15 **Estimate the total revenues of Disney's *Tarzan*.**

Here's where some prior knowledge comes in handy.

Determine:

1. What were movie ticket revenues in the United States for Tarzan?

2. What percentage of worldwide sales is the U.S. revenue?

3. How much does Disney make from video sales?

4. What are Disney's revenues from cross licensing agreements (dolls, posters, etc.)?

AND TRY THESE FOR MORE PRACTICE...

16   How many red cars are there in the United States?

Notes:

17   What is the annual demand for table napkins in the United States?

Notes:

18   How many times would the population of China circle the globe if they held hands?

Notes:

19   What is the size of the poultry market in the United States?

Notes:

20   How many people are cremated in the United States every year?

Notes:

21   How many barbers are there in New Orleans?

Notes:

22 **What is the annual market for peaches in the United States?**

Notes:

23 **What are the revenues of the Plaza Hotel?**

Notes:

24 **How many hotel-size bottles of shampoo and conditioner are produced each year around the world?**

Notes:

Hungry for more inside scoop? Join Vault.com's popular
online community for consulting — www.vault.com

VAULT.COM **129**

BRAINTEASERS

You might be taken aback when your interviewer suddenly asks you: "So, if you were selling a television and your neighbor was selling the identical set for half the price, what would you do?" Or, perhaps, that beloved (by interviewers) chestnut "Why is a manhole round?" Some of these questions have no set answer. Instead, the interviewer is assessing creativity, composure, your ability to deconstruct the problem, and finally your ability to ask directed and relevant questions. Others do have answers, which you are expected to reason out calmly, quickly and logically. "Cases and guesstimates are given to candidates to test reasoning skills, but be warned – brainteasers are sometimes given to test your poise under stress," says one consultant.

Remember...

Brainteasers are very unstructured, so it is difficult to suggest a step-by-step methodology. There is one set rule, though: Take notes as your interviewer gives you your brainteaser, especially if it's mathematical in nature. Other than that, you may select any starting point you are comfortable with, and then ask directed questions around the answers you get back from the interviewer. You may need to break the question down into several parts depending on its complexity, but it is not important to start in any particular place.

Every year consulting firms tell us they discourage the use of brainteasers – and every year we hear about candidates getting them.

PRACTICE BRAINTEASERS

1 Why are manhole covers round?

The classic brainteaser, straight to you via Microsoft (the originator). Even though this question has been around for years, interviewees still encounter it. Here's how to "solve" this brainteaser. Remember to speak and reason out loud while solving this brainteaser!

Why are manhole covers round? Could there be a structural reason? Why aren't manhole covers square? It would make it harder to fit with a cover. You'd have to rotate it exactly the right way. So many manhole covers are round because they don't need to be rotated. There are no corners to deal with. Also, a round manhole cover won't fall into a hole because it was rotated the wrong way, so it's safer.

Looking at this, it seems corners are a problem. You can't cut yourself on a round manhole cover. And because it's round, it can be more easily transported. One person can roll it.

2 The power has gone out in your hotel room and it is pitch black. You have 11 white socks and 10 black socks in your suitcase. (It's a long-term engagement.) You must put on a matched pair of socks, or you'll look terrible at your presentation! How many socks must you pull from the drawer to be assured of a matched pair?

Don't be fooled! Either white or black will do, so you need only three socks to be sure of either a white or black matched pair.

Hungry for more inside scoop? Join Vault.com's popular
online community for consulting — www.vault.com

VAULT.com **133**

3   You are in a room with three light switches. Each controls one of three light bulbs in the next room. You must determine which switch controls which bulb. All lights are off. You may flick only two switches and enter the room with the light bulbs only once. How would you determine which switch controls which light bulb?

This is an invitation from the consulting firm to express your "out-of-the-box" thought patterns. Staring in disbelief, whimpering in fear, or otherwise reacting negatively will shoot down your chances. So be creative. Ask if you can pull out your cell phone and call a pal for assistance. Run out and buy a drill so you can peek through the wall. There is, however, one especially elegant solution. Turn one light bulb on for about twenty minutes. Then turn it off. Turn another switch on. Then enter the room and feel the two bulbs that are off. The hot one will be attached to the switch that you just turned off. Using all your senses – that's thinking like a consultant!

4   You are in a rowboat on a lake with the anchor dropped. You pull up your anchor. Does the water level in the lake rise, lower, or stay the same?

The intuitive answer for many is to say that the water level remains the same – but it doesn't. It rises, becasue the anchor displaces a larger volume of water when it is pulled up and in the boat than when it is on the bottom of the lake.

5 You have 12 balls. All of them are identical except one, which is either heavier or lighter than the rest. The odd ball is either hollow while the rest are solid, or solid while the rest are hollow. You have a scale, and are permitted three weighings. Can you identify the odd ball and determine whether it is hollow or solid?

This is a pretty complex question, and there are actually multiple solutions. First, we'll examine what thought processes an interviewer is looking for, and then we'll discuss one solution. (This question is reportedly in use at McKinsey, incidentally.)

Start with the simplest of observations. The number of balls you weigh against each other must be equal. Yeah, it's obvious, but why? Because if you weigh, say three balls against five, you are not receiving any information. In a problem like this, you are trying to receive as much information as possible with each weighing.

For example, one of the first mistakes people make when examining this problem is that they believe the first weighing should involve all of the balls (six against six). This weighing involves all of the balls, but what type of information does this give you? It actually gives you no new information. You already know that one of the sides will be heavier than the other, and by weighing six against six, you will simply confirm this knowledge. Still, you want to gain information about as many balls as possible (so weighing one against one is obviously not a good idea). Thus, the best first weighing is four against four.

Secondly, if you think through this problem long enough, you will realize how precious the information gained from a weighing is: You need to transfer virtually every piece of information you have gained from one weighing to the next. Say you weigh four against four, and the scale balances. Lucky you! Now you know that the odd ball is one of the unweighed four. But don't give into the impulse to simply work with those balls. In this weighing, you've also learned that the eight balls on the scale are normal. Try to use this information.

Finally, remember that consultants love that out-of-the-box thinking. Most people who work through this problem consider only weighing a number of balls against each other, and then taking another set and weighing them, etc. This won't do. There are a number of other types of moves you can make – you can rotate the balls from one scale to another, you can switch the balls, etc.

Hungry for more inside scoop? Join Vault.com's popular
online community for consulting — www.vault.com

VAULT.com **135**

Let's look at one solution:

For simplicity's sake, we will refer to one side of the scale as Side A, and the other as Side B.

Step 1: Weigh four balls against four others.

Case A: If, on the first weighing, the balls balance

If the balls on our first weighing balance we know the odd ball is one of those not weighed, but we don't know whether it is heavy or light. How can we gain this information easily? We can weigh them against the balls we know to be normal. So:

> **Step 2 (for Case A):** Put three of the unweighed balls on Side A; put three balls that are known to be normal on Side B.

> > **I.** If on this second weighing, the scale balances again, we know that the final unweighed ball, is the odd one.

> > **Step 3a:** Weigh the final unweighed ball (the odd one) against one of the normal balls. With this weighing, we determine whether the odd ball is heavy or light.

> > **II.** If on this second weighing, the scale tips to Side A, we know that the odd ball is heavy. (If it tips to Side B, we know the odd ball is light, but let's proceed with the assumption that the odd ball is heavy.) We also know that the odd ball is one of the group of three on Side A.

> > **Step 3b:** Weigh one of the balls from the group of three against another one. If the scale balances, the ball from the group of three that was unweighed is the odd ball, and is heavy. If the scale tilts, we can identify the odd ball, because we know it is heavier than the other. (If the scale had tipped to Side B, we would use the same logical process, using the knowledge that the odd ball is light.)

Case B: If the balls do not balance on the first weighing

If the balls do not balance on the first weighing, we know that the odd ball is one of the eight balls that was weighed. We also know that the group of four unweighed balls are normal, and that one of the sides, let's say Side A, is heavier than the other (although we don't know whether the odd ball is heavy or light).

> **Step 2 (for Case B):** Take three balls from the unweighed group and use them to replace three balls on Side A (the heavy side). Take the three balls from Side A and use them to replace three balls on Side B (which are removed from the scale).

I.   If the scale balances, we know that one of the balls removed from the scale was the odd one. In this case, we know that the ball is also light. We can proceed with the third weighing as described in step 3b from Case A.

II. If the scale tilts to the other side, so that Side B is now the heavy side, we know that one of the three balls moved from Side A to Side B is the odd ball, and that it is heavy. We proceed with the third weighing as described in step 3b in Case A.

III. If the scale remains the same, we know that one of the two balls on the scale that was not shifted in our second weighing is the odd ball. We also know that the unmoved ball from Side A is heavier than the unmoved ball on Side B (though we don't know whether the odd ball is heavy or light).

Step 3: Weigh the ball from Side A against a normal ball. If the scale balances, the ball from Side B is the odd one, and is light. If the scale does not balance, the ball from Side A is the odd one, and is heavy.

Whew! As you can see from this solution, one of the keys to this problem is understanding that information can be gained about balls even if they are not being weighed. For example, if we know that one of the balls of two groups that are being weighed is the odd ball, we know that the unweighed balls are normal. Once this is known, we realize that breaking the balls up into smaller and smaller groups of three (usually eventually down to three balls) is a good strategy – and an ultimately successful one.

Hungry for more inside scoop? Join Vault.com's popular
online community for consulting — www.vault.com

VAULT.com **137**

6 You are a king, with a hundred princes and princesses in your kingdom. Every year, the princes and princesses must bring you a bag of one hundred gold coins that weigh one ounce each. But you have learned there is a traitor in your realm. He or she will bring you hollowed out coins this year – and then strike at you! You are allowed to do one traditional weighing of coins on a scale. How will you use this opportunity to flush out the traitor?

Various versions of this puzzle have been making the rounds on the brainteaser circuit. "You give back what you get," shrugs one consultant. Here's how to tame this problem (and to reason its solution out loud). First of all, if you ask if you can mark a coin from each prince and princess, your interviewer will tell you no – that would be far too easy! You'll need to find another way to solve this dilemma. The key is that you must find a way to somehow "mark" which prince or princess donates which coin. Number each prince and princess from one to 100. Then tell each to put that number of coins onto the scale. Calculate how much the group of coins should weigh, and determine how many ounces you're short. That number of ounces is also the number of the traitor. Guards!

7 You have a five-gallon jug and a three-gallon jug. You must obtain exactly four gallons of water. How will you do it?

"They gave this question even after *Die Hard with a Vengeance* came out!" says one outraged consultant. But whether you've seen that gimmicky, puzzle-based movie or not, you should find this brainteaser pretty simple. Fill the three-gallon jug with water and pour it into the five-gallon jug. Repeat. Because you can only put two more gallons into the five-gallon jug, one gallon will be left over in the three-gallon jug. Empty out the five-gallon jug and pour in the one gallon. Now just fill the three-gallon jug again and pour it into the five-gallon jug. Ta-da.

8   You are faced with two doors. One door leads to your interview (that's the one you want!), and the other leads to the exit. In front of each door is a consultant. One consultant is from a firm that always tells the truth. The other is from a firm that always lies. You can ask one question to decide which door is the correct one. What will you ask?

Clearly, you can't just ask a consultant which is the correct way – one of them will lie to you. The important thing is to work in a double negative. Ask a consultant: "If I were to ask you if this door was the correct one, what would you say?" The truthful consultant will, of course, answer yes (if it's the correct one) or no (if it's not). Now take the lying consultant. If you asked the liar if the correct door is the right way, the liar will answer no. But if you ask the liar how they would answer if you asked them the same question, the liar will be forced to lie about the fact that they would say no – and answer yes.

Another solution is to ask a consultant: "If I were to ask the other guy which way to go, what would he say?" The reasoning is similar – except in this case, you should go the opposite way.

9   You have 100 black marbles and 100 white marbles. You have two jars into which to place the marbles. You must randomly select a marble, and you wish to maximize your odds of choosing a black marble. How do you distribute the marbles, and what are your odds of choosing a black marble after you make your distribution?

If you place all the black marbles in one jar and all the white marbles in another, your chances will be 50/50. Your best bet is to put one black marble in one jar and all the other marbles in the other one. In the one jar, the chance of picking the black marble will be 100 percent. In the other one, your chance is 49.5 percent. Averaged, your chance of grabbing a black marble is 74.75 percent.

Hungry for more inside scoop? Join Vault.com's popular
online community for consulting — www.vault.com

V/\ULT.com   **139**

FINAL
ANALYSIS

Case questions can be very disturbing if you haven't encountered them before. You may have prepared well for the standard interview questions like "Tell me about yourself," and "Describe your greatest achievement." But case questions stretch your poise, professionalism, analytical abilities, and deductive reasoning power in ways that consultants are asked to perform every day. If you become comfortable with this line of questioning by practicing and preparing, you will be well equipped to meet the difficulty of these questions. Try to have fun with the challenge of the case interview. The more you enjoy solving problems and using your analytic and creative ability, the better you'll do and the more fun you'll have. Good luck – practice, don't be nervous (all interviewers were candidates once), and crush those case interviews!

APPENDIX

Consulting glossary

The consulting industry uses many "buzzwords." Following is a basic list that can raise your level of familiarity with consulting terms. Consultants often lapse into their own lingo while conversing with civilians, thus further panicking those who were unaware that they possessed something called a "skill set" (for what it's worth, the things that you're good at). Here is a short rundown of some of those worlds that consultants like to fling about in case interviews:

Bananagram: A graph showing profitability (the typical measure of profitability for this graph is return on capital employed, or "ROCE" [pronounced roachy]) vs. relative market share. The graph shows that the higher the market share, the higher the profitability.

BCG matrix: A portfolio assessment tool developed by BCG. Also called a growth/share matrix.

Benchmarking: Measuring a value or practice or other business measure (such as costs) against other companies in the industry.

Blank slide: Initial sketch on paper for a slide to be used in a consulting case presentation (called blank because it does not include data until analysts put it in).

Brainteaser: A type of consulting interview question in which the job seeker is asked to solve a logic problem.

Business Process Re-engineering (BPR): BPR is the process of reviewing a client's business processes, eliminating unneeded or "non-value-added" tasks, and then implementing the leaner, more efficient process.

Case team: Team that works on a consulting project for a client. Usually composed of one partner (or director), one consultant, and two or more analysts.

Change management: One of the services provided by consulting firms, in which the firm helps a company cope with a period of significant change (such as a merger, downsizing or restructuring).

Consultancy: A typically European name for what we call a "consulting firm" in the U.S., though the term has picked up currency in the U.S.

Convergence: The trend toward industries uniting. (For example, cable TV customers may someday be able to place telephone calls using cable technology, while telephone customers may be able to receive television through phone lines.)

Core competencies: The areas in which a company excels. Consultants believe a company should enter only those businesses which are part of its core competencies.

Critical path: This term comes from Operations Management theory. Every business process is made up of a series of tasks. Some of these tasks are related to maintenance of the process or administrative and bookkeeping issues. Taken away, they do not directly impact the end result of the business process. If you eliminate these non-meaningful tasks, you are left with the core set of tasks that must occur in order for the process to produce the desired result. This is the critical path. In everyday consulting language, it is used to refer to only those work tasks which are the most important at the time.

DCF: (Discounted Cash Flow). The present value of a future cash flow.

Drilldown: Asking questions to gather more detail about a situation, usually from a high-level (big picture) view.

80/20 rule: Getting 80 percent of the answer first will take 20 percent of your time. The other 20 percent of your time may not be worth it.

Engagement: A consulting assignment received by a consulting firm. Also called a "case" or "project."

Experience curve: The principle that a company's costs decline as its production increases. One assumption used by consultants that a company's costs decline by roughly 25 percent for every doubling in production (e.g. a company's 200th unit of a product costs 75 percent of the 100th unit's cost).

Granularity: This simply refers to the basic elements that make up a business problem. Imagine a handful of sand. At a high level it's simply a handful of sand; at a granular level it is bits of many different kinds of rock and shell matter reduced to fine granules over time by the action of the ocean. Consultants are not usually this poetic.

Hungry for more inside scoop? Join Vault.com's popular
online community for consulting — www.vault.com

VΛULT.com **145**

Guesstimate: A type of consulting interview question. Guesstimates require job seekers to make an educated estimate of something (often the size of the market for a particular product or service) using basic calculations.

Helicoptering: See High-level view.

High-level view: This is also referred to as a "50,000-foot view." It refers to describing a situation in general terms or as an overview of a situation.

Hoteling: Consultants move around so much that in some firms they are not assigned permanent offices, just a voice mail extension. Each week, they must call up the office nearest them to request a desk. This is called "hoteling."

Hurdle rate: A company's cost of capital. In general, if the return on an investment exceeds this "hurdle rate," the company should make the investment; otherwise, the company should not.

Implementation: The process by which a consulting firm ensures that the advice it gives to a client company is enacted.

Learning curve: The rate at which a consultant acquires background information or industry knowledge needed for a case. A "steep" curve is a good thing.

NPV: (Net present value). The sum of a series of discounted cash flows. Used to assess the profitability for a client of making an investment or undertaking a project.

O'Hare test: A test consultants use in interviews to assess personality "fit". If I was stuck overnight with this person at O'Hare airport, would I have fun?

On the beach: For consultants, the spare time between assignments, when their work hours decline drastically. Consultants between assignments are said to be "on the beach" (not literally). This expression originated at McKinsey.

Out-of-the-box thinking: Creativity.

Outsourcing: Taking a process normally performed within a company and hiring an outside vendor to perform the task, often at a lower cost and with better results. Examples of processes that are commonly outsourced include: payroll, data processing, recruitment, and document processing. Outsourcing is a growing trend among corporations.

Reengineering: A largely discredited fad of the early 1990s, which advocates a complete overhaul (and usually downsizing) of a company's strategies, operations, and practices.

Rightsize: Also "downsize," this is just a kinder, friendlier term for restructuring the elements of a company. This is most often used in reference to headcount reductions, but can apply to plants, processes, technology, financial elements, and office locations.

Shareholder value: The wealth of a company's stockholders or their equity (ownership) of the company. The primary goal of consultants in undertaking any engagement is to increase shareholder value.

Stakeholder: A critical person who has a stake in the outcome of a particular situation. Most commonly, the stakeholders in a case are the shareholders, creditors, or employees.

Total Quality Management: Also known as TQM. Management with the purpose or intent of producing a product or offering a service of the highest quality, with zero tolerance for defects.

Value migration: The flow of economic and shareholder value away from obsolete business models to new, more effective designs.

Value-added: Used to define a service or product in a marketplace that adds value to a pre-existing product or way of doing things.

Workplan: A schedule for completing a consulting engagement.

Writing a deck: Preparing slides for presentations to clients.

White space opportunity: An opportunity for a company to make money in an area in which they are currently generating zero revenue (for example, launching a new product line, licensing an existing brand or technology, or entering a new geographic market).

Hungry for more inside scoop? Join Vault.com's popular
online community for consulting — www.vault.com

VAULT.com **147**

Recommended Reading

- Hammer, Michael and James Champy. *Reengineering the Corporation.* New York: Harper Business, 1993.

- McTaggart, James. *The Value Imperative: Managing for Superior Shareholder Returns.* New York: Free Press, 1994.

- O'Shea, James and Chales Madigan. *Dangerous Company: Management Consultants and the Companies They Save and Ruin.* New York: Times Business, 1997.

- Porter, Michael. *Competitive Strategy.* New York: Free Press, 1980.

- Prahalad, C.K. and Gary Hamel. "The Core Competence of the Firm." *Harvard Business Review,* (1990).

- Slywotzky, Adrian. *Value Migration.* Boston: Harvard Business School Press, 1996.

- Stern, Carl and George Stalk, Jr. (ed). *Perspectives on Strategy: from the Boston Consulting Group.* New York: John Wiley & Sons, 1998

Hungry for more inside scoop? Join Vault.com's popular
online community for consulting — www.vault.com

VAULT.com **149**

About the Author

Mark Asher: Mark is a consultant at PricewaterhouseCoopers.